BEST OF

San Francisco

China Williams

Best of San Francisco 2
2nd edition – October 2004
First published – October 2002

Published by Lonely Planet Publications Pty Ltd
ABN 36 005 607 983

Australia	Head Office, Locked Bag 1, Footscray, Vic 3011
	☎ 03 8379 8000 fax 03 8379 8111
	🖳 talk2us@lonelyplanet.com.au
USA	150 Linden St, Oakland, CA 94607
	☎ 510 893 8555 toll free 800 275 8555
	fax 510 893 8572
	🖳 info@lonelyplanet.com
UK	72–82 Rosebery Avenue, London EC1R 4RW
	☎ 020 7841 9000 fax 020 7841 9001
	🖳 go@lonelyplanet.co.uk

This title was commissioned in Lonely Planet's Oakland office and produced by: **Commissioning Editor** Suki Gear **Coordinating Editor** Carly Hall **Coordinating Cartographer** Birgit Jordan **Layout Designer** Steven Cann **Proofer** Simone Egger **Indexer** Carly Hall **Cartographer** Natasha Velleley, Joelene Kowalski **Managing Cartographer** Alison Lyall **Cover Designer** Candice Jacobus **Project Manager** Eoin Dunlevy **Series Designer** Gerilyn Attebery **Mapping Development** Paul Piaia **Regional Publishing Manager** David Zingarelli **Thanks to** Darren O'Connell, Corinne Waddell, Jennifer Garrett, Owen Eszeki, Danielle North

Photographs by Lonely Planet Images, Ray Laskowitz and Anthony Pidgeon except for the following: p48, p68 Jerry Alexander, p42, p83 Glenn Beanland, p60 Jean-Bernard Carillet, p81 Richard Cummins, p23 John Elk III, p47, p49, p94 Lee Foster, p43 Greg Gawloski, p33, p106 Rick Gerharter, p56, p61, p98, p99, p100, p40 Roberto Gerometta, p20, p44 Kim Grant, p19, Richard I'anson, p29, p74 Curtis Martin, p43 Monica Meares, p46 Steve Rosenberg, p103 David Ryan **Cover photograph** Golden Gate Bridge and San Francisco, John Elk III/Lonely Planet Images. All images are copyright of the photographers unless otherwise indicated. Many of the images in this guide are available for licensing from Lonely Planet Images: 🖳 www.lonelyplanetimages.com.

ISBN 1 74059 785 0

Printed through Colorcraft Ltd, Hong Kong.
Printed in China

Acknowledgements © Bay Area Rapid Transit

HOW TO USE THIS BOOK

Color-Coding & Maps

Each chapter has a color code along the banner at the top of the page which is also used for text and symbols on maps (eg, all venues reviewed in the Highlights chapter are orange on the maps). The fold-out maps inside the front and back covers are numbered from 1 to 7. All sights and venues in the text have map references; eg, (3, E1) means Map 3, grid reference E1. See p128 for map symbols.

Prices

Multiple prices listed with reviews usually indicate adult/senior/child (eg $10/7/4) or adult/child (eg $13/6) admission to a venue. Meal cost and room rate categories are listed at the start of the Eating and Sleeping chapters, respectively.

Text Symbols

☎	telephone
✉	address
🖳	email/website address
$	admission
🕙	opening hours
ⓘ	information
Ⓜ	BART
🚇	Muni
⛴	ferry
🚌	auto route
Ⓟ	parking available
♿	wheelchair access
🍴	on site/nearby eatery
👶	child-friendly venue
Ⓥ	good vegetarian selection

Contents

From the Publisher

AUTHOR

China Williams

San Francisco is the only place on the planet off-kilter enough to categorize China Williams as part of the 'mainstream.' Before moving to San Francisco, China grew up in South Carolina and had short affairs with Washington, DC, and Thailand. She is presently on a self-imposed exile in Portland, Maine, where she lives with her husband, Matt. Thanks to Stacey McCarthy, Jonathan Rose and Juliana Cobb for letting me crash their sacred spaces. Many veggie burritos to Suki Gear who brought me back to the Promised Land. Thanks also to Marion Bowler, Unny Han, Drew Keenan, Evan Demik, Mike McCormick, and Michael and Stacy Jean McCarthy. Kudos to Russell H for his art archiving. A shout-out to my homies in the Oakland office. And grand applause to my husband, who tied the knot with me under those SF redwood trees.

The 1st edition of this book was written by Tom Given.

DEDICATION

Our city lost a beloved daughter on July 26, 2004 - Maria Donohoe, wife, mother and dear friend. A rare third-generation San Franciscan, Maria gave up her career in law to share her love of travel with the world. As we marveled at her selfless work ethic and unwavering integrity, she rose from editor to Lonely Planet's US Publishing Manager. Ever graceful, practical and compassionate, Maria treated the world with respect and wonder. We are blessed to have shared in her joy, and she will always inspire us.

PHOTOGRAPHERS

Ray Laskowitz

For photographer Ray Laskowitz, photographing San Francisco was like taking a journey through the past. Although he grew up in Southern California, he studied and began his career in the Bay Area.

Anthony Pidgeon

Oakland-based editorial photographer Anthony Pidgeon has well and truly made San Francisco his home. Moving there from San Diego 13 years ago, Anthony freelances for many local and national publications and is a house photographer for several Bay Area concert venues.

SEND US YOUR FEEDBACK

We love to hear from travelers – your comments keep us on our toes and help make our books better. Our well-travelled team reads every word on what you loved or loathed about this book. Although we cannot reply individually to postal submissions, we always guarantee that your feedback goes straight to the appropriate authors, in time for the next edition – and the most useful submissions are rewarded with a free book. To send us your updates – and find out about LP events, newsletters and travel news – visit our award-winning website: 🖵 www.lonelyplanet.com.

Note: We may edit, reproduce and incorporate your comments in Lonely Planet products such as guidebooks, websites and digital products, so let us know if you don't want your comments. For a copy of our privacy policy visit 🖵 www.lonelyplanet.com/privacy.

Introducing San Francisco

When the scratchy woollen blanket of fog recedes, San Francisco is flooded by pure, undiluted sunlight and a boundless blue sky. In the distance, a vermillion necklace bridge adorns the rugged Marin headlands and San Francisco's thumb-shaped peninsula. From inside the city, uniform white boxes spread down 43 hills like a terraced flowerbed of seashells. Up closer, the boxes are elaborately colored Fabergé eggs with gingerbread trim and buxom bay windows.

This is a city of neighborhoods not of skyscrapers, of possibilities not of privilege, of characters not of pedigree. San Francisco was built by determined misfits – gold miners, out-of-the-closets, hippies and Internet tycoons – who have kindled an inextinguishable spirit of optimism. From the finest restaurants to the grungiest bars, everyone is welcome to cast off the doldrums of Old World conventions and to reinvent themselves (even if only for a day).

This wide-open freedom is hard to resist and more tempting when you see the fog creep over the hills like a stalking tiger, sneak a peek at the sparkling bay from a steeply pitched street or watch a makeshift parade claim a street-side performance space. And when you tire of sight-seeing, the easygoing restaurants will impose memories of intense and refreshing flavors assembled from California's endless bounty. Here's your chance to donate your heart, like so many others, to the City by the Bay.

San Francisco's signature fog rolls in over the Golden Gate Bridge

Neighborhoods

Most tourists find themselves in the northeast pocket of the city with the office towers of the **Financial District** and the tiny shops of **Union Square**. Affluent and busy, downtown will leave East Coasters wondering what all the fuss is about. This district of pompous granite boxes and shadow-casting skyscrapers is merely a prerequisite into the club of elite world cities defined by such elders as New York, London and Paris. Such regimented conformity fits San Francisco like a non-native language always spoken with an accent. The city's real heart and soul is found in the residential neighborhoods with their postcard views and flamboyant houses.

Due north of the Financial District is **Chinatown** and the Italian enclave of **North Beach**, where streets start to take near-vertical leaps into the air and the sparkling bay peeks out between the tall buildings. To the west is **Russian Hill** and to the east is **Telegraph Hill**, both of which are formidable ascents for flatlanders. At the foot of these hills is **Fisherman's Wharf**, where clam chowder, overpriced T-shirts and sea lions prevail. The **Embarcadero** follows the bay from here down to the Ferry Building shops and SBC Park.

The artery of Market St slices through the **Tenderloin**, a seedy district characterized by junkies, prostitutes and a hardworking community of Southeast Asian immigrants. Directly across from Market St is the flatlands of **South of Market (SoMa)**, home of the homeless and computer geeks, flophouses and countless dance clubs. It slides into the Latino neighborhood of the **Mission**, partially claimed by artists and neo-punk hipsters.

Near the crown of Market St, the rainbow flag serves as the welcome mat to the **Castro**, one of the country's most famous gay and lesbian neighborhoods. Next door is the district known as the **Haight**, divided into the traditionally African American area around the **Fillmore** and **Lower Haight** (between Market St and Divisadero), and the old hippie haunt of **Upper Haight** (west of Divisadero). Haight St terminates at **Golden Gate Park**, which ends its meandering run at the tumultuous Pacific Ocean.

Off the Beaten Track

Tired of waiting in line for the cable cars or driving miles out of your way because left turns have been outlawed? You are in need of two-wheeled liberation – a bicycle (see p115 for rentals). Cruise along the Embarcadero or around Golden Gate Park (p14). For 'in-the-know' views of the Golden Gate Bridge, head to Baker Beach (p36), or as an alternative to crowded Twin Peaks, head to Corona Heights (p36).

Itineraries

San Francisco's most charming aspects are its unexpected vistas and quirky neighborhoods. It is a walkable city, crisscrossed by public buses, with plenty to see and do. The **CityPass** (www.citypass.com, $40) includes admission to five museums and cable car fares; and most museums are open late on specific nights with reduced admission.

DAY ONE
Wander through Chinatown and North Beach to Fisherman's Wharf for the ferry to Alcatraz. Alternatively, do the Russian Hill High walking tour (p44) or the Bay to Bridge bike tour (p41). Ride the F line streetcar or either of the Powell cable cars. Dine downtown in the Financial District or around Union Square, or head to North Beach. For nighttime antics, head to North Beach or catch a play at one of the downtown theaters.

DAY TWO
The avant-garde awaits at the San Francisco Museum of Modern Art (p26) and the Yerba Buena Center (p26). Foreign-culture junkies should opt for the Asian Art Museum (p9). Head to the Mission for lunch and a public art tour (p49). Finish with a night at the opera or symphony, an outing to the dance clubs and music venues in South of Market, or a bar crawl through the Mission or the Castro.

DAY THREE
Head to the Haight for shopping and post-hippie revivals then wander through Golden Gate Park. Go for lunch at Ebisu (p76). Don't forget about the view from Twin Peaks or Lincoln Park. Eat and drink on Haight St.

Worst of San Francisco
- Getting caught outdoors when the cold fog comes home
- Sprinting for the bus and watching it roll away
- Back-of-the-bus comedians and trash-talkers
- Haight St's panhandlers hailing from the wealthy Marin suburbs

Highlights

ALCATRAZ (3, E1)

The country's most famous prison enjoys one of the most beautiful settings and, in turn, exacted the cruellest form of torture on its inmates. Ordinary life – a woman's laughter, the smell of the old Ghirardelli chocolate factory, sailboats and streetcars – was close enough to taunt the prisoners. Freedom was only a mile away, but the icy waters controlled by invisible currents were more treacherous than a life sentence. Only three inmates ever took the plunge, escaping from 'the Rock' in 1962 on a self-made raft; they were never seen again.

Alcatraz was a derelict military installation in the 1920s, when the federal government turned it into a maximum security, escape-proof prison for the toughest cons. Famous residents include Al Capone, 'Machine Gun' Kelly and Robert Stroud (the so-called Bird Man of Alcatraz). Opened mainly as a publicity stunt to show the country that the government was tough on crime, Alcatraz was closed in 1963 as a financial disaster – housing an inmate here carried the same price tag as a night at New York's Waldorf Astoria hotel.

INFORMATION

- ☎ 705-5555
- 🖥 www.blueandgold fleet.com
- ✉ ferries leave from Fisherman's Wharf Pier 41
- $ day tours $16/14.25/10.75, evening tours $23.50/21/14.25
- ⏱ ferries 9:30am-2:15pm, also Thu-Sun 4:20pm
- ℹ make reservations early, opt for the audio tour and bring warm clothes
- 🚌 F line to Pier 41
- ♿ yes
- ✕ Ferry Building Marketplace (p77)

Six years after the closure of the prison, a group of Native Americans occupied the abandoned island, claiming the Rock for Indians of all tribes. They held the island for almost two years, drawing media attention and law-enforcement scrutiny. Federal marshals removed the last protesters in 1971, paving the way for conversion of the island into a national park.

DON'T MISS

- The cell used for solitary confinement (known as 'the hole')
- Effigies of the Anglin brothers used to fool the guards for their escape
- Graffiti left behind by Native American protesters
- The view of the city

Freedom looms large behind Alcatraz

ASIAN ART MUSEUM (5, A7)

This bombastic beaux art building, the former main library, is an unlikely place to find great treasures from the Buddhist nations of the world. But fittingly the museum reflects the nearness in demographics of San Francisco's population to its cross-Pacific neighbors, and the prestige of the collection – one of the country's largest. Over 15,000 objects represent almost every culture in Asia and span over 6000 years. The collection is grouped first by geography and further into religious works then cultural handicrafts. Explanatory signs walk visitors through the regional dialects of Buddhist iconography, from the sensuous Indian sculptures to the reserved Chinese representations. The Southeast Asian collection fo-

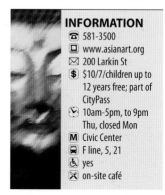

INFORMATION

☎ 581-3500
🖳 www.asianart.org
✉ 200 Larkin St
💲 $10/7/children up to 12 years free; part of CityPass
🕐 10am-5pm, to 9pm Thu, closed Mon
Ⓜ Civic Center
🚌 F line, 5, 21
♿ yes
🍽 on-site café

cuses primarily on the serene figures of Thailand with a few pieces from the great Khmer empire.

The secular art is most impressive in the Chinese section where a glass frame mounts a collage of illuminated jade and an impressive assembly of Chinese bronzes. In fact Chinese art accounts for about a third of the permanent collection. Unique to this museum is the small gallery of Sikh art, the only display of its kind in the US. Korea is also given prominence in its own right. Indonesian reed puppets and ritual weapons, and ancient Japanese pottery and textiles bring aesthetic enjoyment even if fatigue results in only an appreciative nod. The ground floor galleries exhibit contemporary Asian art, which bring the collection's historical elements into the present.

DON'T MISS

- Korean celadon from Goryeo dynasty
- Traditional Japanese tearoom
- Thai paintings
- Oldest known Chinese Buddha

Feast your eyes on more than 6000 years of history at the Asian Art Museum

CABLE CARS (5, C6 & D4)

San Francisco's emblematic cable cars turn mundane transportation into a promenade. From the standing room along the exterior to the wooden bench facing the pedestrian traffic, the world slides by at 9mph with a cacophonous symphony of grinding brakes, clanging drive cables and the bell announcing stops. Up and over the city's enormous hills, the cable cars invoke a childlike thrill in grown adults who hoist themselves aboard with clumsy determination.

INFORMATION

- ☎ 673-6864
- 💻 www.sfmuni.com
- ✉ downtown turntable at Powell & Market Sts (5, C6) and California & Market Sts (5, D4)
- 💲 $3; one-day pass $9; part of CityPass
- 🕑 6:30am-12:30am
- ℹ Cable Car Barn Museum (p29)
- Ⓜ Powell St or Embarcadero
- ♿ yes
- ✕ Sears Fine Food (p69) or Buena Vista

Feel the wind in your hair – at 9mph

Cable cars were invented here in the 1870s by Andrew Hallidie, a Scottish engineer. He figured if you could pull a bucket of ore out of a mine shaft, you could pull a streetcar full of people up a hillside. He laid out a five-block test track on Clay St, using a continuous underground loop of cable that the car would grip for acceleration and release for deceleration. The experimental line worked and a network of 100 miles of tracks subsequently crisscrossed the city.

San Francisco began abandoning lines in the 1940s, igniting a preservation movement that ultimately saved three lines. Those three lines – the **California St** line from Market St to Van Ness Ave; the **Powell-Mason** line from Union Square to North Beach and Fisherman's Wharf; and the **Powell-Hyde** line from Union Square over Russian Hill to Ghirardelli Square and Aquatic Park – were completely rebuilt in the 1980s. Queues are long on the Powell cable cars, the California St line is less crowded.

Commuting in Style

When the cable cars were closed for renovations in the 1980s, Muni began running its 1950s streetcars along Market St, the historic thoroughfare for electric trolleys. The vintage revival was so successful that Muni acquired other retired streetcars from cities across the world, including the venerable Streetcar Named Desire from New Orleans. The historic F line now runs from the Castro along Market St to the Embarcadero and Fisherman's Wharf.

THE CASTRO (4, A2)

Synonymous with 'coming out,' the Castro was a refuge for gay men and women from all over the country. It was a place where gay couples could live together openly, where singles could cruise without fear of retaliation and where the gay rights movement of the 1970s and '80s matured.

INFORMATION

- ✉ roughly bounded by Church, 14th, Eureka & 19th Sts
- ℹ Cruising the Castro walking tour (p49)
- 🚎 K, L, M lines to Castro station, F line, 22
- ♿ yes
- ✕ Café Flore (p63)

In the 1950s, the Castro was a working-class neighborhood of mostly Irish and Italian immigrants, with pubs and parochial schools. As the families moved to the suburbs, gay men began moving in, attracted at first by cheap rents and then by all those other gay men. By the mid-1970s, the streets teemed with hordes of young men in tight jeans, flannel shirts and moustaches (the Castro clone look).

With a distinct identity, the Castro rallied politically around Harvey Milk, who became the first openly gay man to be elected as a city official. Milk ran his campaign out of his camera shop at 575 Castro St – now memorialized by a sidewalk plaque and mural. Milk was fatally shot by a fellow supervisor in 1978.

The heyday of the Castro District as a liberator has declined in recent years because the neighborhood's higher rents have dispersed the younger generation into the city at large. But the Castro's legendary sexual energy and penchant for performance is still unleashed, particularly on a sunny day and at its favorite festivals – the **Castro St Fair** (p80) and **Halloween** (p80).

Attitude and style in the Castro

The Quilt that Remembers

The Castro was spiritually and physically devastated by the AIDS epidemic in the 1980s and early '90s, which was responsible for 20,000 deaths citywide. Fearing that the victims would be forgotten, activists started the AIDS Memorial Quilt, composed of handmade name memorials. Families across the country added panels and the quilt grew to be the largest community art project in the world, covering the entire mall in Washington, DC, at its last public display. The quilt now resides in Atlanta.

CHINATOWN (5, C4)

Chinatown is two parallel worlds – a theme village façade that is palatably exotic and a private interior that is incongruously foreign. The Fisherman's Wharf of Chinatown, **Grant Ave** is lined with souvenir shops as authentically Chinese as fortune cookies (a San Francisco invention). Along **Stockton St** real life ensues with pungent smells and crowded markets where housewives poke at live chickens or gasping fish. The elders assemble in **Portsmouth Square** (segregated by gender) to play checkers and gamble.

Traditional Chinese building, Chinatown

Many of the first Chinese immigrants came to San Francisco as gold prospectors and laborers on the transcontinental railroad in the mid-18th-century. Regarded with hostility by the White majority, the Chinese established a fortress-like ethnic enclave. To conduct business and help new immigrants, the predominately male population (Chinese women were barred from immigrating by the Chinese Exclusion Act of 1882) organized family associations – including the enduring and prestigious **Chinese Six Companies** (843 Stockton St). The notorious underworld of the early 20th century was ruled by *tongs* (or gangs) operating brothels and opium dens along Chinatown's numerous **alleys** (Beckett, Ross and St Louis). Today these alleys are sunless chambers of cramped apartments with laundry hanging out to dry.

Chinatown survives today as an intact community because new immigrants have arrived to replace integrated families. Most of the original settlers were Cantonese from southern China, joined later by anti-communists fleeing the revolution. As of late, the red flag of the People's Republic now appears (ever so rarely) alongside the Republic of China flag. If you're after an insider's view of Chinatown, the **Chinese Culture Center of San Francisco** (☎ 986-1822; 750 Kearny St, 2nd fl, Holiday Inn; $17/8; 10:30am Wed, 10:30am & 1pm Sat) conducts historical walking tours.

DON'T MISS

- Golden Gate Fortune Cookie Bakery (☎ 781-3956; 56 Ross Alley; ⏱ 10am-7pm)
- Chinese New Year Parade (p80)
- Chinese Historical Society of America (p29)
- Pacific Heritage Museum (p31)
- Sun Yat-sen Memorial (p32) in St Mary's Square

FISHERMAN'S WHARF (5, A1)

Like every seaside resort, Fisherman's Wharf is a scruffy mix of carnival attractions, chain restaurants and souvenir stands. Tourists are magnetically drawn here no matter how much their local friends protest. To the Wharf's credit, it is easy to navigate, and the local characters (including the sea lions and the panhandlers) are quintessential San Francisco.

Fisherman's Wharf was once a working waterfront, but after WWII seafood restaurants were clearly more profitable than fishing. Today the Wharf covers about 10 blocks. At the eastern end, **Pier 39** is a faux–New England fishing village with stores and restaurants. Nearby are the real celebrities of Fisherman's Wharf – the **sea lions** who sunbathe on the abandoned marina between Pier 39 and 41. On land these clumsy creatures bark and pose for pictures like attention-hungry starlets. This is a good spot to hit late afternoon to see the commuting fog return home through the span of the Golden Gate Bridge and stealthily engulf the city.

The city's maritime history is recognized with two collections of **historic ships** ($7/5/4; 9am-6pm Sun-Thu, to 8pm Fri & Sat). Pier 45 features the only surviving WWII Liberty ship in working order and a WWII submarine. The **Hyde St Pier** ($5; 9:30am-5pm) is home to 19th-century sailing ships and ferries that operated in the San Francisco harbor. **Aquatic Park**, at the tail-end of Fisherman's Wharf, is the city's only bay-front beach and home to the **Maritime Museum** (p30).

DON'T MISS

- The Bush Man panhandler
- Swimmers at Aquatic Park
- Venetian Carousel and Aquarium of the Bay (p39) at Pier 39
- Whimsical Musée Mécanique (p31)

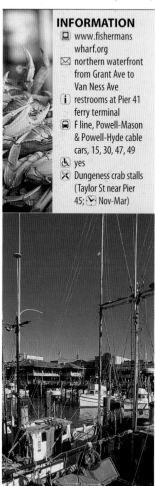

INFORMATION

- www.fishermanswharf.org
- northern waterfront from Grant Ave to Van Ness Ave
- restrooms at Pier 41 ferry terminal
- F line, Powell-Mason & Powell-Hyde cable cars, 15, 30, 47, 49
- yes
- Dungeness crab stalls (Taylor St near Pier 45; Nov-Mar)

Maritime mayhem at Fisherman's Wharf

GOLDEN GATE PARK (2)

Designed as an urban playground, Golden Gate Park has become an informal stage for the city's wacky exhibitionists. On a sunny weekend, when the park is closed to motor vehicles, all the characters come out to play in their favorite costumes – spandex bicyclists looking like futuristic robots, old-school roller skaters practising disco moves, and ragtag drummers on Hippie Hill invoking the spirit of the Summer of Love. The manic spectacle is protected from the outside world by a thick green belt of Monterey pines and cedars whose gnarled branches ceremoniously hold up the cloudless blue sky (between periods of fog). Interspersed between are the shaggy eucalyptus trees whose leaves perfume the air as potently as the skunky-smelling cigarettes passed among friends.

All this happens in a rectangle about 3 miles long and less than 1 mile wide. And hardly a stitch of the lush natural covering is authentic. In the 1870s this was a barren stretch of windswept sand dunes leading to the Pacific Ocean until the city transformed it into gardens, winding roads, and picnic and sport facilities. Interestingly, the planners were inspired by New York City's Central Park, designed by Frederick Law Olmsted, who gave a no-confidence vote to San Francisco's sandy dreams.

Entering the park at John F Kennedy Dr is the **Conservatory of Flowers** (☎ 666-7001; John F Kennedy Dr; $5/3/1.50; 🕑 9am-5pm Tue-Sun), a Victorian-era greenhouse displaying orchids, giant water lilies and reflections of misty rainbows projected from the stained glass ceiling. Originally brought from Ireland in 1876 for millionaire James Lick, the conservatory was acquired by the park and opened to the public until 1995 when it was badly damaged during a storm. A massive restoration project has returned the

INFORMATION

- ☎ 831-2700
- ✉ bounded by Stanyan St, Fulton St, Lincoln Way & the Great Highway
- $ free
- 🕑 sunrise to sunset
- ℹ visitor center (1000 Great Hwy, lobby of Beach Chalet; free walking tours; 🕑 9am-6pm)
- 🚌 N line, 5, 7, 29, 44, 71
- ♿ yes
- ✗ Park Chow (2, D3; ☎ 665-9912; 1238 9th Ave, Sunset); Beach Chalet (p32); Good Luck Dim Sum (p76)

Take in Golden Gate Park at your own pace

conservatory to working order. Directly across from the conservatory is a stone bridge with such lovely acoustics that neighborhood musicians perform impromptu serenades to delighted onlookers. Heading westward are the **California Academy of Sciences** (p39, closed until 2008) and the **De Young Museum** (p29), both of which flank the Music Concourse and band shell (for more contrived performances).

Beside the De Young Museum is the mysteriously popular **Japanese Tea Garden** (☎ 666-7001; Hagiwara Tea Garden Dr; $3.50/1.25, cash only; ⏱ 8:30am-5pm), a 5-acre folly built for the Midwinter Exposition in 1892 and tended by the Hagiwara family until they were interned after Pearl Harbor. The small sandbox of dwarf trees and Buddhist replicas are certainly cheaper than a visit to Japan, but seem rather forced, especially on a crowded day.

> **DON'T MISS**
> - The imperial philodendron in the Conservatory of Flowers
> - Dahlia Garden in summer
> - National AIDS Memorial Grove
> - Gigantic ferns across the road from the Conservatory
> - White uniformed lawn bowlers

If you can bear the disappointment from friends back home, skip the tea garden and head straight for the **Strybing Arboretum & Botanical Gardens** (☎ 666-7001; Martin Luther King Jr Dr; free; ⏱ 9am-4:30pm Mon-Fri, 10am-5pm Sat & Sun), a living museum of plants. An ancient stand of redwoods, a garden of fragrance, California natives and desert succulents provide enough roaming room to smell the flowers.

The remainder of the park is geared to residents but does hold a few worthwhile sites best reached by bicycle rather than foot. The city's most famous Wyoming transplants occupy the **bison paddock**, where the native American herd sleeping in the sun look more like tree stumps than the charging creatures of frontier lore. Following the road almost to the end will deliver you to the **Dutch windmill** and **Queen Wilhelmina Tulip Garden**, the park's last gasp before reverting back to its origins as sand dunes and scraggly pines. At the end of the road, the gunmetal grey Pacific Ocean pounds against the submissive expanse of **Ocean Beach**. A good stopping point is the **Beach Chalet** (p32), which is decorated with 1930s murals and has an upstairs dining room with a spectator's view of the ocean.

Embrace the view from the traditional wooden bridge in the Japanese Tea Garden

GOLDEN GATE BRIDGE (3, B1)

San Francisco Bay's iconic pendant, the Golden Gate Bridge, is elegantly pinned between the stern headlands and the competing expanse of the sky and the ocean. Named after the hue of the surrounding hills at sunset, the Golden Gate Bridge was erected one fluted tower at a time beginning in 1933. Although the topography seems suited to a span bridge, construction logistics required creative engineering. Before the bridge took on its familiar shape, a submerged but watertight fender was built to keep out the powerful tides so that the two towers could be anchored into the bedrock floor. When it was opened in 1937 to a pedestrian-only crowd, San Franciscans applauded the work of Joseph Strauss, the bridge's promoter, and Irving and Gertrude Morrow, the designers, as well as the riveters, divers and other locals who executed the plans.

The Golden Gate Bridge has a near perfect figure – 1.7 miles long, 746ft tall (for each suspension tower) and the unique vermillion color of 'international orange,' which blends with the natural environment. In contrast to most big bridges, the Golden Gate was designed as much for people as for cars. Wide pathways on either side of the bridge accommodate pedestrians and bicyclists who come for the views of the wild ocean and the city streets.

INFORMATION

- ☎ 921-5858
- 🖥 www.goldengate bridge.org
- ✉ I-101/Hwy 1
- 💲 pedestrians & bicyclists free, autos $5 going south
- 🕑 pedestrian access 6am-6pm Nov-May, 5am-9pm Apr-Oct
- ℹ gift shop at southeast side open 9am-5pm Sep-May, 8:30am-7:30pm Jun-Aug
- 🚌 28, 29 to pedestrian entrance, Golden Gate Transit bus 76 across the bridge on Sun and some holidays
- ♿ yes
- 🍽 Bridge Café (🕑 9:30am-5pm Sep-May, 9am-7pm Jun-Aug)

Traverse San Francisco's golden icon

The Bridge's Makeup Artists

Like an adored movie star, the bridge receives ongoing attention from a crew of 55 ironworkers and painters to undo the damage from wind, fog and time. Traversing the heights and depths of the bridge by foot, the crew removes corroded panels and repaints exposed surfaces – all by hand.

THE HAIGHT (2)

Documented ad nauseam, the Haight-Ashbury of the 1960s could romantically be described as a youth utopia. Part hedonism, part social revolution, this once run-down neighborhood hosted the convergence of mind altering drugs like LSD, a distaste for the status quo and lots of disaffected teenagers. If what they say is true, everything was free – drugs, sex and rock and roll. And longhaired, freaky people – including rock legends Janis Joplin, the Grateful Dead, Jefferson Airplane, and LSD-guru Ken Kesey – were there on the streets with all the other Haight-Ashbury hippies. By the 1967 Summer of Love, the trip was ending thanks to increasing drug overdoses and violence, and too many people wanting a piece of the peace sign.

INFORMATION
- ✉ centers around Haight & Ashbury Sts
- ☺ stores 11am-7pm, bars 5pm-2am
- 🚌 N line, 6, 7, 22, 24, 33, 71
- ♿ yes
- ✕ Citrus Club (p69)

Today the old Victorian homes are million dollar showpieces, a Gap and Ben & Jerry's occupy the famous Haight and Ashbury Sts corner, and pricey shoe stores outnumber head shops. Even the neighborhood's name has changed to 'the Haight' (only aging flower children still call it 'Haight-Ashbury'). A lot hasn't changed, though – teenagers still run away to the Haight to do drugs and panhandle. An anti-establishment idealism still persists too – former hippies hand out food and neighbors organize to block chain stores from moving in. The Haight's streets are also filled with shrines to the past, from the sidewalk gardens dedicated to deceased rock stars to the psychedelic paintings for sale in the lobby of the **Red Victorian Bed, Breakfast & Art** (p102).

DON'T MISS
- Haight walking tour (p43)
- Amoeba Records (p57)
- Haight St Fair (p80)

Stepping out on popular Haight Street

LINCOLN PARK & SUTRO BATHS (2, A1)

Lying between Golden Gate Park and the Presidio, Lincoln Park is a little bit of Big Sur inside San Francisco city limits. Along the serpentine coastline, craggy rocks punctuate the endless expanse of ocean beating furiously at the unyielding cliffs and coves. This natural spectacle is aided in its beauty by the charismatic fog, which elicits the melancholy moan of the foghorns during its daily assault on the city. In the distance a container ship plods its way to Asia.

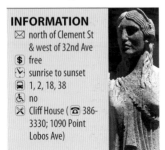

INFORMATION

- ✉ north of Clement St & west of 32nd Ave
- 💲 free
- ☼ sunrise to sunset
- 🚌 1, 2, 18, 38
- ♿ no
- ✗ Cliff House (☎ 386-3330; 1090 Point Lobos Ave)

During the city's early career, this far-flung area was considered wasteland, too foggy and sandy to attract anyone but squatters and drifters. Adolph Sutro, a former mayor with a sizable fortune, ignored common wisdom and purchased the area known as **Sutro Heights** (within present-day Lincoln Park), where he built a cliffside home and turned the coastal section into a Victorian-era amusement center. Only the footprints remain of Sutro's most popular attraction, the **Sutro Baths**, the world's largest indoor swimming pool. This gaudy complex boasted a faux Grecian temple entrance, seven pools (six saltwater and one freshwater), viewing galleries and an oddities gift shop. People loved the place, at least until times and tastes changed; in 1966 it was destroyed by a fire.

DON'T MISS

- Camera Obscura beside the Cliff House (p38)
- Palace of the Legion of Honor (p31)
- Coastal Trail to Land's End

Today narrow footpaths zigzag from the Sutro Heights parking lot around the ruins and rugged terrain of the park. When exploring these wild corners, stick to the **Coastal Trail** and remember to never turn your back on the Pacific Ocean as rogue waves frequently exact human tribute.

Memories of a bygone era, the Sutro Baths

THE MISSION (4)

A trip to the Mission will make the rest of San Francisco seem like a sleepy hamlet. Charged with an unpredictable energy, the Mission is fueled by an urban grittiness and brassy Mexican ballads. The streets are littered with life – the heroin zombies around 16th and Mission, the sulking hipsters around Valencia St, and the squeaky clean Latino families wheeling fat babies home after a trip to the *bodegas* (markets). The druggies, immigrants and modern-day bohemians create a diverse, often inharmonious, urban experience.

The Mission is San Francisco's oldest settlement. Five days before the American colonists declared

INFORMATION

- ✉ main thoroughfares include Valencia, Mission, 16th & 24th Sts
- Ⓜ 16th St & 24th St
- 🚌 J line, 22, 26, 33, 47, 48, 49
- ♿ yes
- 🍴 Taquería Pancho Villa (p72)

independence, Father Junipero Serra consecrated **Mission Dolores** (☎ 621-8203; 3321 16th St; $3/2; 🕙 9am-4pm Nov-Apr, 9am-4:30pm May-Oct), the sixth in a chain stretching up the coast of Spain's new frontier. The permanent structure, with 4ft adobe walls, survived the 1906 earthquake and is San Francisco's oldest building. The adjacent cemetery contains an incomplete record of the mission's early residents. A statue of an Indian maiden commemorates the unmarked graves of the Ohlone Indians who built the mission, and surviving headstones remember Luis Antonio Arguello (first Mexican governor) and other notables.

The settlement around Mission Dolores became a working-class neighborhood of mostly Irish and Italian immigrants in the 1850s. Latinos (mainly Mexicans) repopulated the Mission as the country's labor demographics changed dur-

DON'T MISS

- · Mission murals (p42)
- · Southern Exposure gallery (p34)
- · La Rondalla (p82)
- · Eating a Mission burrito (p72)

ing the 1960s. Latino arts are on display at the **Mission Cultural Center for Latino Arts** (☎ 821-1155; www.missionculturalcenter.org; 2868 Mission St; $2; 🕙 10am-4pm Tue-Sat). Situated on the district's eastern fringes, the abandoned factories became yet another center of counter-culture with off beat artists' studios and experimental theaters, many of which were shoved over to the East Bay by the short-lived dot.com boom.

PACIFIC HEIGHTS (6, B3)

Contradictory to San Francisco's egalitarian spirit, there is a blue blood aristocracy concentrated in the hillside mansions of Pacific Heights. To the

INFORMATION

✉ west of Van Ness to the Presidio, south of Union to California

🚌 22, 30, 41, 45, 47, 49

🍴 Betelnut (p75)

The dollhouse-like Haas-Lilienthal House

modern eye, the perfectly preserved Victorians seem like exquisite dollhouses for a royal family of giants. Washington St, which runs beside Alta Plaza and Lafayette Park, is one of the best (and steepest) streets for taking a house-envy stroll. Historic tours of the **Haas-Lilienthal House** (p27) and the **Octagon House** (p27) are available to the public. Commanding a spectacular view of the bay, they say, **Spreckels Mansion** (p28) is a massive edifice now belonging to romance novelist Danielle Steele (who says love can't pay the rent?).

The rich or aspiring take themselves on outings to the shopping and entertainment streets of Union and Fillmore. The beautiful people congregate here in large cliques reminiscent of college fraternities and sororities. In a fascinating reenactment of TV soap operas or dating shows, ambition and lust are obvious and tangible even to a clueless outsider.

Self-made Silver Spoons

Alma de Bretteville Spreckels (1881–1968) was born poor but possessed good looks and a regal-sounding name. She exposed enough of herself (literally) to attract sculptor Robert Aitken, who used her as the model for the Victory figure atop Union Square's (p37) monument to Admiral Dewey. Once rendered in bronze, she married into the wealthy Spreckels family, sealing her fate as a headline-making socialite. She chain-smoked, reached for martinis instead of water and founded the Palace of the Legion of Honor (p31).

See Alma de Bretteville Spreckels' legacy at the Palace of the Legion of Honor

THE PRESIDIO (3, C2)

The Presidio is a most unusual park. It undertook a dramatic career change in 1994 from being a military base to a National Park Service site.

And it is enormous – 1480 acres, more than double the size of New York's Central Park. As you would expect, there is plenty of nature worth exploring (including the Coastal Trail). But unlike most parks, the Presidio has mixed use with civilian housing, business offices and a highly secretive, yet very visible, special effects complex for Lucasfilm Entertainment Company.

Like a natural gatekeeper, the point of land occupied by the Presidio was destined to be a military fort. The Spanish spotted this in 1776 and the Americans wrestled it from the Mexicans in 1846. Fearing an attack during the Civil War, the US Army built **Fort Point** (☎ 556-1693; Marine Dr; free; 🕙 10am-5pm Fri-Sun), a triple-tiered fortress at the mouth of the bay. The fort never saw action from the beleaguered Confederates, and it is now a museum with a phenomenal view of the Golden Gate Bridge.

In the interior of the park, the **San Francisco National Cemetery** serves as the final resting ground for soldiers from the Civil War to the present. Equally interesting is the **pet cemetery** which was first used to bury army guard dogs and later family pets. Homemade signs, like 'Skipper, the best damn dog we ever had – 1967,' add a living voice to the park's otherwise forlorn mood of abandoned buildings and memorials.

INFORMATION

- ☎ 561-4323
- 🖥 www.nps.gov/prsf
- ✉ temporary visitor center at Officer's Club, Bldg 50, Moraga Ave; permanent site to open 2007 at Bldg 102, Montgomery St
- 💲 free
- 🕙 sunrise-sunset; visitor center 9am-5pm
- 🚌 28, 29, 43
- ♿ yes
- ✕ Warming Hut Café (☎ 561-3040; Marine Dr)

DON'T MISS

- Palace of Fine Arts (p29)
- Exploratorium (p39)
- Baker Beach & Battery Chamberlain (p36)
- Surfers in front of Fort Point

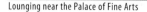

Lounging near the Palace of Fine Arts

NORTH BEACH & TELEGRAPH HILL (5, C3)

In the northeastern corner of San Francisco, North Beach rises head-strong from the bay to the rocky peak of Telegraph Hill. It is a lively neighborhood cut from European cloth and sewn in the free-spirit style of California. On a sunny day people crowd the sidewalks and sip cappuccinos in Italian-esque **sidewalk cafés**. At night the neon lights eclipse the sky and revelers emerge to dance and drink with Gold Rush–era abandon.

INFORMATION

- ⊠ bounded by Broadway, Grant Ave, Chestnut St & Sansome St
- $ Coit Tower $3.75/ 2.50/1.50
- ☺ Coit Tower 10am-6pm
- 🚌 30, 39
- ℹ summer weekends are crowded; be prepared to queue for the elevator up Coit Tower
- ✗ Mario's Bohemian Cigar Store Café (p73)

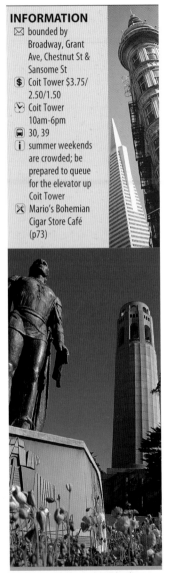

Coit Tower and Christopher Columbus battle to dominate Telegraph Hill

During the 1840s gold prospect-ors and vagabonds unloaded at the neighborhood's feet – around the area bounded by Pacific Ave, Sansome, Washington and Kearny Sts – with a lust for wealth, women and wine. Labelled the Barbary Coast, the pre-landfill shore dotted with red brick buildings was the city's primary red-light district of bordellos and burlesque shows.

Subduing forces eventually built a working-class neighborhood re-ferred to as the Latin Quarter for its large number of Italian and Span-ish immigrants. The focal point of the transplant community and surviving generations is a dandy twin-spired Catholic church, **Sts Peter & Paul**, which served as the wedding picture background for baseball star and native son Joe DiMaggio and his new bride Mari-lyn Monroe. (The actual wedding was held in City Hall since both were divorced.)

Bohemian artists and poets of the 1950s – including Jack Kerouac and Allen Ginsberg – found the cheap rents liberated them from the nine-to-five routine, and in the coffee shops and bars they created a youth revolution known as the Beat movement. Their rebel yell took the form of poetry with the backup of avant-garde jazz music. With succeeding generations, counterculture migrated to the Haight, leaving North Beach a gentrified ghetto with bohemian sensibilities. Today the artistic undercurrent survives thanks to poet Lawrence Ferlinghetti and his **City Lights Bookstore** (p57), the country's first paperback bookstore and publisher of Ginsberg's controversial poem *Howl*.

A steep climb up Telegraph Hill, along Filbert St, leads past a cascade of bay windows and pastel-colored houses reflecting the honest California sun. Standing sentinel on the hill is the 210ft fluted **Coit Tower**, named after its financier, Lillie Hitchcock Coit. As a child in San Francisco, little Lillie loved the city's fire department and was an honorary member of the Knickerbocker Engine Company No 5. Adulthood brought Lillie a little money and a rebellious streak, resulting in a posthumous endowment to the city to build a beautifying monument. Despite Lillie's fascination with fires and the unarguable resemblance of the tower to a fire hose nozzle, the history books claim that the monument was designed merely as an observation point. That it does – you can see Mt Tamalpais to the north, the graceful Golden Gate Bridge to the west and the masculine San Francisco–Oakland Bay Bridge to the east, but best of all you might

A touch of Europe in North Beach

catch an impromptu cocktail party on a nearby apartment roof deck.

In the tower's lobby is an equally spectacular site: Depression-era murals depicting California life and industries. Painted by 25 local artists, the murals have a unifying style and even a little communist controversy (notice the Karl Marx book in the library scene).

Barenaked Ladies

Strip clubs of all calibers congregate near the intersection of Broadway and Columbus Ave, each trying to outdo the other in neon and scantily clad barkers. The clubs aren't a recent invention of corroded morals but a holdover from the city's rough-and-tumble Barbary Coast days. In the 1960s, the **Condor Club** (Columbus Ave & Broadway) repackaged sexual liberation for the working man in the form of topless dancers; to some the name Carol Doda and her silicone-enhanced buddies might ring a bell. Now the Condor is a fully clothed sports bar with only historic photographs to document the days of yore.

Still bearing all for the skin trade is **Lusty Lady** (☎ 391-3126; 1033 Kearny St), the only female owned, unionized strip club in the country, as well as others with less reputable credits.

SBC PARK (5, E7)

Not every sight in San Francisco is an artifact from the past. SBC Park (formerly and still colloquially called Pac Bell Park) is a smart baseball stadium honoring the scale of an old-fashioned ballpark with all the techy trappings of the Silicon Valley and a picturesque waterfront location.

INFORMATION

- ☎ 972-2400 (park tours)
- ▯ www.sfgiants.com
- ✉ 24 Willie Mays Plaza, btwn 2nd & 3rd Sts
- $ $10/8/5
- ◷ tours 10:30am & 12:30pm
- ⓘ game tickets, see p95
- 🚌 F line, 10, 15, 30, 45
- ♿ yes
- ✗ Acme Chophouse (p77), Red's Java House (p77)

Like most major league ballparks built since Baltimore debuted Camden Yards, SBC Park seats the spectators close to the field and can only handle a relatively small crowd of 41,000. Behind the retro warehouse façade is a high-tech facility with wi-fi networks (for pre-ordering gourmet concessions such as sushi) and electronic ticketing systems. The stadium designers finally noticed San Francisco's peculiar weather patterns and oriented the park with its back to the winds and facing the warmer East Bay. A shallow porch in the right field makes it easier for sluggers (like Barry Bonds) to knock home-runs into the bay, where fans with boats and pet retrievers pounce on breakaway souvenirs.

Take me out to the ball park...

Bleacher Bums

If you want to catch a glimpse of a Giants game but can't score tickets, there is a free standing room section accessible from the waterfront promenade that runs behind the right field fence. It is built into the right field wall and offers an unobstructed view at ground level. Get there early as this spot isn't a secret.

TWIN PEAKS (3, D4)

Forming a striking climax in the San Francisco skyline, Twin Peaks provides the mother of all views in a city filled with spectacular views. From the top of the peaks (a little over 900ft), a 360-degree vista sweeps from the ocean to Golden Gate Park, to the East Bay and across to the southwestern mountains. The scene becomes even more stunning in the dark of night when the city lights become an earthly Milky Way of blinking constellations.

Twin Peaks also cuts a striking figure from the lowlands as the lonely Spanish explorers no doubt noticed when they named the perky peaks 'El Pecho de la Chola' (Breasts of an Indian Girl). Stuck like a pitchfork on a hill beside Twin Peaks is the three-pronged Sutro Tower, an oddly artistic TV and radio antennae. As the day transpires, the gray mass of fog spills over the sculpted peaks into the valley below and swallows up all but Sutro's pointed crown.

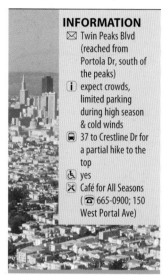

INFORMATION

- ✉ Twin Peaks Blvd (reached from Portola Dr, south of the peaks)
- ℹ expect crowds, limited parking during high season & cold winds
- 🚌 37 to Crestline Dr for a partial hike to the top
- ♿ yes
- ✗ Café for All Seasons (☎ 665-0900; 150 West Portal Ave)

The San Francisco skyline from Twin Peaks

Vista Secrets

San Franciscans have their own 'undiscovered' views where they take out-of-town guests to show off their fair city. We'll let you in on a few:

- Corona Heights (p36)
- Rooftop of the San Francisco Art Institute (p34)
- 33 bus from the Haight to the Mission
- Vallejo Parking Garage (5, B3; 755 Vallejo St at Columbus Ave; Muni 15, 30)

YERBA BUENA ARTS DISTRICT   (5, C6)

San Francisco gladly embraces modern art like a comrade in arms. The revolutionaries meeting hall is the **SFMOMA** (San Francisco Museum of Modern Art; ☎ 357-4000; www .sfmoma.org; 151 3rd St; $10/7/6, free 1st Tue of every month, half price Thu after 6pm, part of City-Pass; ☯ 11am-5:45pm Fri-Tue, 11am-8:30pm Thu), an eye-catching abstract structure. SFMOMA specializes in American abstract expressionists including Clyfford Still, Willem de Kooning and Jackson Pollock, as well as European painters like Pablo Picasso, Henri Matisse and Paul Klee.

The regional galleries follow Richard Diebenkorn and the Bay Area Figurative school, as well as Robert Arneson's cheeky ceramics and Wayne Thiebaud's pop art candy counters. The photography rooms boasts Ansel Adams' stunning black-and-white landscapes, Dorothea Lange's haunting shots of migrant workers and Edward Weston's sensual forms of California's naked hills. The most prized pieces include Diego Rivera's *The Flower Carrier*, Jackson Pollock's *Guardians of the Secret* and Henri Matisse's *Femme au Chapeau*.

Across 3rd St is SFMOMA's unofficial art scout, the **Yerba Buena Center for the Arts** (☎ 978-2787; 701 Mission St at 3rd St; $6/3; ☯ 11am-5pm Tue-Sun), a gallery and theater. Mining for art where art snobs feign to go, Yerba Buena has hosted shows on video games, graffiti and innovative installation pieces. The theater presents performances ranging from Greek tragedy to spoken word.

The museums also form the nucleus of an ambitious development project known as **Yerba Buena Arts District** aiming to bring art and culture within steps of the Moscone Convention Center. Promoters herald this as the 'new San Francisco,' even though it feels as awkward as a junior high dance.

INFORMATION

- ✉ Yerba Buena Arts District bounded by Mission, Folsom, 3rd & 4th Sts
- 💻 www.yerbabuena arts.org
- Ⓜ Powell St
- 🚌 any Market St bus, 14, 26, 30, 45
- ♿ yes
- 🍴 Caffe Museo at SFMOMA

Get in touch with your artistic side in the Yerba Buena Arts District

Museum Row

South of Market isn't the prettiest part of town, but there are a lot of museums here and more are coming. If you have some time to burn in this area, take your pick:

- Cartoon Art Museum (p29)
- California Academy of Sciences (p39)
- Contemporary Jewish Museum (p29)
- Metreon (p40)
- Mexican Museum (p30)
- Zeum (p40)

Sights & Activities

NOTABLE BUILDINGS & LANDMARKS

Bank of Canton (5, C4)
This pagoda-style building was originally a telephone exchange with operators speaking over four Chinese dialects. Now it's a bank – not worth going inside but interesting from the outside.
☎ 421-5215 ✉ 743 Washington St $ free ☀ 9am-4pm Mon-Fri, 9:30am-1pm Sat ☐ 1, 15, 30, 45 ♿

City Hall (5, A7) Viewed from the city's western eyrie, the beaux arts dome of City Hall sits like a regal crown of the gold country empire. The building is regarded as one of the country's best examples of its architectural style.
☎ docent tours 554-6023, art exhibit line 252-2568 ☐ www.ci.sf.ca.us/city hall ✉ 400 Van Ness Ave $ free ☀ building 8am-8pm Mon-Fri, noon-4pm Sat, tours 10am, noon & 2pm Tue-Fri, 12:30pm Sat Ⓜ Civic Center ☐ 5, 19, 21, 49 ♿

Columbus Tower (5, C4)
With its patina turret, this wedge-shaped building (also known as the Sentinel Tower) puffs its chest like a fighting cocky unaware that it is dwarfed by the nearby Transamerica Pyramid (p28). It now houses Francis Ford Coppola's film company and is closed to the public.
✉ 916 Kearny St ☐ 15, 41

Flood Mansion (5, B5)
Built atop Nob Hill, the Flood Mansion (1886) is the only surviving estate of the Bonanza kings, former saloon keepers and miners who struck silver in the Comstock Lode. It now houses the elite Pacific Union Club. Closed to the public.
✉ 1000 California St ☐ California St cable car

Haas-Lilienthal House (6, C3) Made of redwood and reflecting a combination of Victorian styles, this home was built for William Haas, a German immigrant and wholesale grocer, in 1886. It was inherited by his daughter Alice Lilienthal who lived here until her death in 1972.
☎ 441-3004 ☐ www .sfheritage.org ✉ 2007 Franklin St $ $8/5 ☀ tours noon-3pm Wed & Sat, 11am-4pm Sun ☐ 1, 12, 47, 49 ♿ no

Hallidie Building (5, C5)
Breaking the monotony of downtown office buildings, the historic 1918 Hallidie has a cool green glass façade, framed with elaborate fire escapes. The first glass curtain-wall building in the US (a pioneering style from Berlin), the Hallidie was designed by Willis Polk, a prominent San Francisco architect. Closed to the public.
✉ 150 Sutter St Ⓜ Montgomery St ☐ 2, 3, 4, 15, 30, 45

Lombard St (5, A3) The 1000 block of Lombard St is famously known as the 'world's crookedest street' thanks to eight, flower-filled switchbacks. With a 27% grade, the zigzags were added to help cars summit the steep hill.
✉ btwn Hyde & Leavenworth $ free ☀ 24hr ☐ Powell-Hyde cable cars ♿ limited

Octagon House (6, C2)
Even in the 19th century, Californians were health nuts. Built in 1861 to increase the interior sunlight (considered to combat illness), this eight-sided house is one of two survivors of a

Flood Mansion, built atop Nob Hill in 1886

citywide fad. It is now owned by the National Society of Colonial Dames and houses a collection of colonial and federal antiques.

☎ 441-7512 ✉ 2645 Gough St $ donations accepted ☷ tours noon–3pm 2nd & 4th Thu and 2nd Sun of month 🚌 41, 45, 47, 49 ♿ no

Palace of Fine Arts (3, C2)
Bernard Maybeck built this faux Grecian temple for the Panama-Pacific Exposition of 1915. Angled on a lake with the sun perfectly poised above it, the marvel became a favorite for a promenading public and later for shutterbugs. The Exploratorium (p39) is housed within a portion of the building.

✉ Palace Dr at Bay St $ free ☷ sunrise-sunset 🚌 28, 30 ♿

Spreckels Mansion (6, C3)
Looking more like a bank than a house, Spreckels Mansion was built by sugar baron Adolph Spreckels. It's now the private home of novelist Danielle Steele. A tall hedge blocks views of most of the house, but the high security gate does allow a glimpse of her fleet of luxury cars. Closed to public.

✉ 2080 Washington St, across from Lafayette Park 🚌 1, 12

Transamerica Pyramid (5, C4) San Francisco's tallest building stands at 853ft (48 stories). Completed in 1972, the tower covers the stomping grounds of Mark Twain, Bret Harte and Robert Louis Stevenson. One story claims that Twain met a fellow named Tom Sawyer on this block. Closed to public.

✉ 600 Montgomery St Ⓜ Montgomery St 🚌 10, 15, 30, 41

Know Your Painted Ladies

Named after Queen Victoria of England (1837–1901) in the heyday of the empire, the florid style of Victorian architecture found devoted fans in San Francisco's emerging middle class. The examples that survived the devastating 1906 earthquake and fire were the equivalents of tract housing. To increase floor space and light, architects used convex windows, now known as bay windows. As woodworking evolved, so did the Victorians, divided here into three basic flavors:

- **Italianate (1870s)** A plain, false façade with straight roofline and bracketed cornices; 120-126 Guerrero St (4, B1)
- **Eastlake or Stick (1880s)** Square bay windows with straight vertical (or stick-like) adornments around windows and cornices; **Parker House** (6, B5; Scott & Fulton, across from Alamo Sq)
- **Queen Anne (1890s)** Rounded tower with witch's cap and horizontal ornaments like curlicues; Alamo Square's 'Painted Ladies' (6, B5; p36).

MUSEUMS

Cable Car Barn Museum (5, B4) This is the barn where the cable cars come home at night. It's also the home of the engines that turn the cables that pull the cars up and over the hills. ☎ 474-1887 🖳 www .sfcablecar.com ✉ 1201 Mason St 💲 free ⏱ 10am-6pm Apr-Sep, 10am-5pm Oct-Mar 🚃 Powell-Mason & Powell-Hyde cable cars, 1, 30, 45 ♿

California Historical Society (5, D6) The official state historical society has a small exhibition space of paintings and decorative arts. The bookstore's diverse selection is the most interesting drawcard. ☎ 357-1848 🖳 www .californiahistoricalsociety .com ✉ 678 Mission St 💲 $3/2 ⏱ 11am-5pm Tue-Sun Ⓜ Montgomery St 🚌 any Market St bus, 14, 15, 30 ♿

Cartoon Art Museum (5, D6) Underground (or self-published) comics flourished in San Francisco's 1960s hippie culture, turning the superhero genre of DC and Marvel into adultonly satires. Of the day's leading cartoonists, R Crumb is among other Bay Area artists featured here. With financial backing from dearly departed illustrator Charles Schulz, creator of '*Peanuts*,' the museum also curates exhibitions on mainstream comics and local newspaper strips. ☎ 227-8666 🖳 www .cartoonart.org ✉ 655

Mission St 💲 $6/4/2, discounted admission 1st Tue of month ⏱ 11am-5pm Tue-Sun Ⓜ Montgomery St 🚌 any Market St bus, 14, 15, 30 ♿

Chinese Historical Society of America (5, B4) From railroad laborers to city officials, the history of the Chinese in San Francisco unfolds in the old Chinese YWCA designed by Julia Morgan (the Berkeley architect who built the castle for William Randolph Hearst). The museum's quality displays touch on interesting historical tidbits, like the cost of an 1860s passage from Hong Kong to San Francisco (a whopping $55), as well as legislation and immigration issues. ☎ 391-1188 🖳 www .chsa.org ✉ 965 Clay St 💲 $3/2/1 ⏱ noon-5pm Tue-Fri, noon-4pm Sat & Sun 🚃 Powell-Mason & Powell-Hyde cable cars, 1, 30 ♿

Contemporary Jewish Museum (5, E4) This museum presents changing exhibits about Jewish culture and life in a variety of media. In 2007 it will move to much larger quarters in the former Pacific Gas & Electric substation, which will be modified by famed architect Daniel Libeskind (who designed the controversial Jewish Museum in Berlin and was selected then passed over to design the new World Trade Center in New York). ☎ 591-8800 🖳 www .jmsf.org ✉ 121 Steuart St 💲 $5/4/free ⏱ noon-6pm Sun-Thu Ⓜ Embarcadero 🚃 F line, 1, 12, 14, 21, 41 ♿

De Young Museum (2, D2) The collection of art from Africa, the Pacific, and the Americas will rejoin public appreciation in October 2005. ☎ 863-3330 🖳 www .thinker.org ✉ John F Kennedy Dr, Golden Gate

Car pulleys at the Cable Car Barn Museum

Park ⓢ free admission 1st Wed of month ⓒ 9:30am-5pm Tue-Sun, to 8:45pm 1st Wed of month ⓡ 5, 33, 44

Fort Mason Center (6, B1)
Swords have been thoroughly beaten into plowshares at this former military installation used during WWII and the Korean War. Today Fort Mason houses museums, cultural centers, performance groups, and nonprofits. Daily classes offer a cross section of San Francisco's leftward leanings — music for newborns and Zen kung fu. Special events include the annual beer and wine festivals. Individual museums are marked on the map. ☎ information 441-3400 🖳 www.fortmason.org ✉ Laguna St at Marian Blvd; visitor center Bldg 201 ⓢ admission varies; museums free 1st Wed of month ⓒ office 9am-5:30pm Mon-Fri, 9am-5pm Sat & Sun; most museums 11am-5pm Wed-Sat ⓡ 10, 22, 28, 30, 49 ♿

International Museum of GLBT History (5, D6) This museum and archive is the city's official historian of gay, lesbian, bisexual and transgender issues. The archives, viewable by appointment, contain the first lesbian quarterly *Vice Versa* (1947) and an early dildo collection. The museum's inaugural exhibit was dedicated to slain supervisor Harvey Milk. ☎ 777-5455 🖳 www.glbthistory.org ✉ 657 Mission St, Suite 300 ⓢ $4/2 ⓒ 1-5pm Tue-Sat Ⓜ Montgomery St ⓡ any Market St bus, 14, 15, 30 ♿

Maritime Museum (6, C1)
This art deco structure was originally the bathhouse for swimmers at Aquatic Park. It is now the dry land portion of the national historic park. Exhibits document the city's maritime history with historic photos of drunken yachtsmen, salty sailors and figureheads (respectfully clad, of course). The museum also hosts demonstrations of chantey and sailor songs. ☎ 447-5000 🖳 www .maritime.org ✉ Beach &

Polk Sts ⓢ free ⓒ 10am-5pm ⓡ Powell-Hyde cable car, 19, 30, 47, 49 ♿

Maritime Museum Historic Ships (6, C1) The historic ships that make up the maritime park include *Balclutha*, an iron hull square-rigger built in Scotland in 1886. The *Balclutha's* neighbors are the 1890 ferry *Eureka*, which used to carry cars and commuters from Hyde St to Sausalito; the 1895 *CA Thayer*, thought to be the last commercial sailing ship to run from a West Coast port; the 1914 *Eppleton Hall*, a side-wheel tugboat; and the 1891 *Alma*, a flat-bottomed scow. ☎ 447-5000 🖳 www .maritime.org ✉ Pier 41, Fisherman's Wharf ⓢ $5 for 7-day pass ⓒ 10am-5pm ⓡ Powell-Hyde cable car, 19, 30, 47, 49 ♿

Mexican Museum (6, B1)
Showcasing Mexican art from pre-Columbian, colonial and modern times, this museum started life in the Mission but migrated to the Fort Mason

---

Left Coast Lingo

Want to fit in like a local? Well daddy-o, you need to know the lingo.

- *Back door* — Not shorthand for bedroom antics, this phrase is used on the older Muni buses to request the driver to open the back door for exiting passengers.
- *The City* — Humphrey Bogart's pet name for the city, 'Frisco' has lost favor among modern residents. Today only tourists call it 'Frisco' and only New Yorkers call it 'San Fran.' You'll be safe with 'San Francisco' or 'the City.'
- *Green Party* — It may sound like a euphemism for a medical marijuana club, but this left wing political party is a legitimate affiliation for San Francisco's uniquely aligned mainstream.
- *Gough* — Pronounced like 'cough,' this street was self-named by a milkman who served on the city commission to christen city streets.

A Museum for *Vertigo*

In Alfred Hitchcock's classic *Vertigo*, a minor character stole the show – San Francisco. Cast as a pretty backdrop, the cityscapes were so well integrated with the twisting plot that the fantasy became inseparable from reality. Retracing the character's steps across the city would take you to the **Palace of the Legion of Honor** (p31), where Kim Novak's character meditated in front of Carlotta Valdez's portrait. The tomb of Carlotta Valdez stood inside the **Mission Dolores cemetery** (p19), but the headstone was only a prop. The shoreline near **Fort Point** (p21) where Novak jumped into the water was real, and so was the **York Hotel** (p101), which posed as the crummy hotel where Novak resurfaced as a shop girl.

Center. In 2006-2007, the museum will graduate to an even larger facility next door to the new Contemporary Jewish Museum in South of Market (5, C6).
☎ 202-9700 🖳 www .mexicanmuseum.org ✉ Fort Mason Center, Bldg D 💲 $3/2 🕒 11am-5pm Wed-Fri 🚌 10, 22, 30, 47 ♿

Musée Mécanique (5, A1)
A whimsical collection of early-20th-century arcade games, Musée Mécanique is a better waste of quarters than a Vegas slot machine. Risque Mutoscope motion pictures ('See what the belly dancer does on her day off!'), self-playing pianos and a fully operational opium den are just some of the ingenious folk art masquerading as coin operated entertainment.
☎ 386-1170 ✉ Pier 45, Fisherman's Wharf

💲 free 🕒 10am-8pm
🚌 F line, Powell-Mason & Powell-Hyde cable cars, 15, 30, 39, 47 ♿

Pacific Heritage Museum (5, C4) Housed in the former subtreasury building, this museum offers a pleasant stroll through a disjointed collection of exquisite Chinese artifacts and furniture, a small coin collection and a view into the building's now defunct vault.
☎ 399-1124 ✉ 608 Commercial St 💲 free 🕒 10am-4pm Tue-Sat 🚌 California St cable car, 1, 10, 15, 41 ♿

Palace of the Legion of Honor (2, B1) San Francisco's fine arts museum, the Legion of Honor is a work of art in itself, a beaux arts edifice overlooking a spectacular view of the city. The highlights of the collec-

tion includes a wood-and-gilt ceiling carved in Moorish patterns from a Spanish chapel and a Rodin rotunda of cool marble figures.
☎ 863-3330 🖳 www .legionofhonor.org ✉ 34th Ave, north of Clement St 💲 $8/6/free 🕒 9:30am-5pm Tue-Sun 🚌 18 ♿

Wells Fargo History Museum (5, C4) This museum traces the history of Wells Fargo Bank, which was founded in 1852 to provide banking and express mail to the new state of California. A Wells Fargo stagecoach from 1865 is the peach of the collection, other exhibits sketch the 1849 Gold Rush.
☎ 396-2619 ✉ 420 Montgomery St 💲 free 🕒 9am-5pm Mon-Fri Ⓜ Montgomery St 🚌 California St cable car, 10, 15 ♿

PUBLIC ART

Balmy Alley (4, C3) An open-air gallery of murals stretches from one end of this narrow block to the other. Drawing on Mexican muralist traditions, most panels deal with political activism. Breaking away from the traditional style, '*RPsycho City*,' by Sirron Norris, uses a comic book look to depict the view from the artist's apartment. Many of the murals were sponsored by **Precita Eyes Mural Arts Center** (p49), which conducts weekend tours.
✉ off 24th St btwn Folsom & Harrison Sts $ free ☼ sunrise-sunset Ⓜ 24th St ▤ 9, 12, 27, 48 ♿

Beach Chalet (2, A3) Lucien Labaudt, a French-born painter, used frescoes to decorate the ground floor of this historic building. His snapshot of San Franciscans at play in the 1930s, sponsored by the Works Progress Administration (WPA), shows that the clothing styles have changed, while the pursuits have stayed the same. The carved wooden railing of mermaids and sea creatures will lead you to the second floor restaurant (☎ 386-8439; dishes $15; ☼ 9am-10pm).
☎ 386-8439 ▯ www .beachchalet.com ✉ 1000 Great Hwy $ free ☼ 9am-10pm ▤ 5 ♿

Rincon Center (5, E5) This art deco building was the main post office for 50 years. Twenty-nine Depression-style murals in the lobby depict the history of California. The atrium, added during renovation in the 1980s, updates the story with murals of Californian life in the late-20th-century.
☎ 777-4100 ✉ 101 Mission St $ free ☼ 7am-11pm Ⓜ Embarcadero ▤ F line, 1, 14, 21, 41 ♿

Sun Yat-sen Memorial (5, C5) Resembling a something of a folk art religious icon, this steel sculpture depicts Sun Yat-sen, the Chinese revolutionary who helped undermine the last Chinese dynasty (Manchu) in the early 20th century. Founder of the Kuomintang party, Sun Yat-sen served briefly as China's president and is one of the country's few unifying political figures. Beniamino Bufano, a charismatic San Francisco–based sculptor of the 1930s and '40s, designed this statue.
✉ St Mary's Square, Grant Ave & California St $ free ☼ sunrise-sunset ▤ all cable car lines, 30, 45 ♿

Mission School Murals

Latino mural traditions helped inspire the elevation of graffiti and tagging into a distinctive art movement, known as the 'Mission School.' In the 1990s young artists painted abandoned alleys, construction site barriers and sides of buildings using street art styles. Cartoonish and irreverent, many murals recorded the ousting of artists during the Mission's short-lived courtship with Internet start-ups.

- **Clarion Alley** (4, C2; Valencia St btwn 17th & 18th Sts) A defining example of the scene, this dingy alley of druggies and prostitutes is also filled with top-notch murals by CAMP (Clarion Alley Mural Project) artists.
- **Generator Mural** (4, C2; 18th & Lexington Sts) On the side of the Apartment store, this Dr Seuss–influenced mural was painted by Andrew Schoultz.
- **One Tree** (5, B9; 10th & Bryant Sts) Artist Rigo uses street sign motifs to poke fun at the surrounding environment. In this case, the entrance to the freeway is augmented by the huge black-and-white sign pointing out a lone tree.
- **Redstone Hall** (4, C 2; 2948 16th St) The lobby of this former union hall is painted with CAMP murals, including the droopy-eyed characters Barry McGee and Aaron Noble's labor history scene.

San Franciscans at play in a Depression-era fresco by Lucien Labaudt at the Beach Chalet

Wave Organ (6, A1) Stuck at the tip of a jetty, this environmental sculpture is a chamber of carved granite blocks salvaged from an old cemetery. Erected to capture the sound of the waves at high tide, several 'listening tubes' and a 'stereo booth' create a subtle music akin to the noises of a seashell. 🖳 www.exploratorium .edu/visit/wave_organ .html

✉ end of Yacht Rd off Marina Blvd, btwn two marinas, nearest cross streets are Baker & Lyon Sts 💲 free 🕒 24hr 🚌 28, 30 ♿ no

Women's Building (4, B2) Painted by seven female artists, *MaestraPeace* is a vibrant mural of a feminine universe. On the Lapidge St side of the building, Rigoberta

Menchu (a Mayan woman who was awarded the 1992 Nobel Peace Prize) is depicted at the crown holding two mother goddesses. Pick up a key to the murals from within the building where nonprofits work on women's issues. ☎ 431-1180 🖳 www .womensbuilding.org ✉ 3542 18th St Ⓜ 16th St 💲 free 🚌 J line, 14, 26, 33 ♿

GALLERIES

Crown Point Press (5, D6) Crown Point is a gallery, print shop and school rolled into one. It first produced fine arts portfolios for Richard Diebenkorn and Wayne Thiebaud in 1965. Now it is highly regarded for revitalizing the medium of etchings, which are showcased in its gallery space. ☎ 974-6273 🖳 www .crownpoint.com ✉ 20 Hawthorne Lane, off Folsom btwn 2nd & 3rd Sts, 💲 free 🕒 10am-6pm Tue-Sat Ⓜ Montgomery St 🚌 10, 12, 15, 76 ♿

Galería de la Raza (3, E4) At the center of the Latino cultural scene since the early 1970s, Galería de la Raza presents work that speaks to contemporary cultural and political life. ☎ 826-8009 🖳 www .galeriadelaraza.org ✉ 2857 24th St 💲 free 🕒 noon-6pm Wed-Sat Ⓜ 24th St 🚌 9, 12, 27, 48 ♿

Gallery Paule Anglim (5, C5) Young talent graduates from the city's streets and studios into this

experimental gallery. Previous shows have spotlighted locals Barry McGee and Rigo, as well as Louise Bourgeois and Tony Oursler. The works rarely make you think, 'I could do that.' ☎ 433-2710 🖳 www .gallerypauleanglim.com ✉ 14 Geary St 💲 free 🕒 10am-5:30pm Tue-Fri, 10am-5pm Sat Ⓜ Montgomery St 🚌 F line, any Market St bus, 38 ♿

John Berggruen Gallery (5, C5) One of the most famous in the city, this gallery presents a range of modern paintings, drawings and sculpture by American and European artists such as Richard Diebenkorn and Mark di Suvero, and some less well-known.

☎ 781-4629 ⌨ www
.berggruen.com ✉ 228
Grant Ave $ free
🕙 9:30am-5:30pm Mon-Fri, 10:30am-5pm Sat
Ⓜ Montgomery St
🚃 F line, 9, 30, 45 ♿

Hackett-Freedman Gallery (5, C5) No abstract impressionists here. Michael Hackett and Tracy Freedman focus on representational work, but have recently expanded to include Bay Area moderns such as Hans Hoffman and his rosebud-lipped women in bold colors.

☎ 362-7152 ⌨ www
.hackettfreedmangallery
.com ✉ 250 Sutter St,
4th fl $ free
🕙 10:30am-5:30pm
Tue-Fri, 11am-5pm Sat
Ⓜ Montgomery St
🚃 F line, any Market St
bus, 15 ♿

Rena Bransten Gallery (5, C5) Contemporary and cutting edge perspectives are represented here in paintings, photos and videos. The gallery's base of funk artists (a San Francisco movement of mixed media) sets the tone for a more current collection of raw or campy artists, including John Waters, Tracy Moffatt and Vik Muniz.

☎ 982-3292 ⌨ www
.renabranstengallery.com
✉ 77 Geary St, 2nd fl
$ free 🕙 10:30am-5:30pm Tue-Fri, 11am-5pm
Sat Ⓜ Montgomery St
or Powell St 🚃 F line, any
Market St bus, 15 ♿

San Francisco Art Institute (5, A2) This Mission revival building has defined Bay Area art for 130 years. Ansel Adams founded the school's photography department, and sculptor faculty member Beniamino Bufano got fired for being too radical. (In one story, he cut off his finger and mailed it to President Wilson to protest WWI.) There are two galleries (Walter & McBean Gallery and Diego Rivera Gallery) where student art is displayed. The Rivera gallery is so named because of a permanent fresco by the famed Mexican muralist.

☎ 771-7020 ⌨ www
.sfai.edu ✉ 800 Chestnut
St $ free 🕙 11am-6pm
Mon-Sat 🚃 Powell-Mason & Powell-Hyde
cable cars, 30 ♿

SF Camerawork (5, B8) This nonprofit has showcased photography and related work by emerging and established artists for more than 25 years.

☎ 863-1001 ⌨ www
.sfcamerawork.org
✉ 1246 Folsom St
$ free 🕙 noon-6pm
Tue-Sat 🚃 12, 19 ♿ no

Southern Exposure (3, E4) This space was originally used to display work by artists affiliated with Project Artaud, San Francisco's oldest live-work space. Set deep in the artsy wilds of the Mission, Southern Exposure has now grown into an independent nonprofit that has helped catapult emerging artists into the local radar.

☎ 863-2141 ⌨ www
.soex.org ✉ 401 Alabama
St $ free 🕙 11am-5pm
Tue-Sat 🚃 12, 22, 27, 33
♿

How Live-Work Didn't Work

New York City artists in SoHo pioneered the reclamation of abandoned factories as studios in the 1970s – a trend that migrated to the forgotten factories of San Francisco. In the late '80s, the ever helpful city government legitimized the phenomenon by adjusting zoning laws to encourage live-work cohabitation. All was peaceful until the Internet economy brought new demand for mixed use buildings, and lots of cash to pay for it. Suddenly live-work lofts were profitable, throwing the city into a well-rehearsed drama between the haves and the have-nots. Artists were evicted to make room for telecommuting Silicon Valley programmers and e-commerce start-ups. Within a few short years, however, Media Gulch turned into Tumbleweed Alley, and the boom went bust like the Gold Rush before it.

HOUSES OF WORSHIP

Glide Memorial Church (5, B6)
As the story goes, Reverend Cecil Williams asked God for help tending to the needy in the Tenderloin, and God told him to do it himself. Today Glide is an only-in-San Francisco institution that offers scores of programs for the neighborhood as well as Sunday gospel services with psychedelic slide shows that draw people from all over the city.
☎ 771-6300 ⌨ www
.glide.org ✉ 330 Ellis St
$ donations accepted
☺ service 9am Sun
Ⓜ Powell St 🚌 27 ♿

Grace Cathedral (5, B5)
Some churches are just for praying, while others provide entertainment. This 20th-century version of a Gothic cathedral crowns the nob of Nob Hill and offers plenty of spectacles – psychedelic stained glass windows, the copy of the Gates of Paradise from the Baptistery in Florence and meditative Labyrinth Walks.
☎ 749-6300 ⌨ www
.gracecathedral.org
✉ 1100 California St
$ $5 ☺ 8am-6pm
Mon-Sat, 7am-7pm Sun, services daily 🚌 California St cable car ♿

Holy Virgin Cathedral (2, C1)
The onion domes of this cathedral stand guard over the Russian Orthodox community of the Richmond, settled here since the days of White Russians. The icons, incense and relics, such as the body of St John of Shanghai and San Francisco, are treasured keepsakes.
☎ 221-3255 ✉ 6210 Geary Blvd $ donations accepted ☺ 11am-1pm, also open for services 8am & 6pm 🚌 38 ♿ limited

Kong Chow Temple (5, C4)
This Chinese temple boasts an altar and statuary carved in Canton. The temple's central deity is Kuan Di, symbolic of strength and education.
☎ 788-1339 ✉ 855 Stockton St, 4th fl
$ donations accepted
☺ 10am-4pm
🚌 30, 45 ♿

Old St Mary's Cathedral (5, C4)
The first Catholic cathedral in the city was built in 1854. Its stout walls survived the earthquake and fire in 1906, though the bells and altar were melted. A small exhibit of historic photos line the foyer.
☎ 288-3800
✉ 660 California St
$ donations accepted
☺ 7am-7pm Mon-Fri, 7am-4pm Sat, services daily 🚌 California St cable car, 1, 15, 30, 45 ♿

San Francisco Zen Center (6, C5)
The oldest Buddhist monastery in the US offers residential meditation retreats at one of three northern California locations, including this San Francisco institution. You can also drop by to help make soup or distribute food to the homeless.
☎ 863-3136 ⌨ www
.sfzc.com ✉ 300 Page St
$ free ☺ 9:30am-5pm Mon-Fri, 9am-noon Sat
🚌 6, 7, 21, 66, 71 ♿

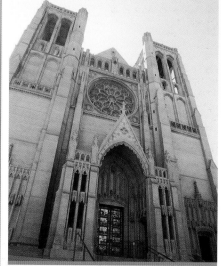
Expect entertainment and prayer at the Grace Cathedral

St Mary's Cathedral (6, C4)
With its daring parabolic lines, the cathedral looks like a space shuttle momentarily posing on a pedestal before blast off. The wide-angle view of Twin Peaks and the city from the inside, plus the ultramodern design of aluminium and stained glass will leave you dumbfounded.
☎ 567-2020 ✉ 1111 Gough St $ donations

accepted 🕓 6:45am-4:30pm Mon-Fri, 6:45am-6:30pm Sat, 7:15am-4:45pm Sun, services daily
🚌 38, 47, 49 ♿

Vedanta Temple (6, B2)
Five domes, representing various world religions, crown the roof of this unusual Pacific Heights Victorian building. Established as

a Hindu temple in 1906, the organization has since moved to a larger temple nearby at 2323 Vallejo St, but it is still in use for lectures and other events.
☎ 922-2323
✉ 2963 Webster St
$ donations accepted
🕓 call for weekly services in the new Vallejo St temple
🚌 22, 30, 41, 45 ♿ no

PARKS & BEACHES

Alamo Square (6, B5)
Sitting at a steep pitch, Alamo Square park provides a pleasant platform for viewing the famous postcard view of a row of Victorian houses with the downtown skyscrapers in the background.
☎ 831-2700 ✉ bounded by Hayes, Steiner, Fulton & Scott Sts $ free
🕓 sunrise-sunset
🚌 5, 21, 22, 24 ♿

Angel Island (3, D1) With 12 miles of hiking and biking trails, and fresh bay breezes, Angel Island provides a quick and scenic getaway from city business. The island's varied history – it has served as a military base, an immigration station, a WWII Japanese internment camp, and a Nike missile site – is still visible today.
☎ 435-1915 💻 www .angelisland.org
$ admission free, ferry ticket $12/6.50/free
🕓 one daily morning departure from Pier 41, Fisherman's Wharf and one afternoon return from Angel Island, three

departures each way on summer weekends
⛴ Blue & Gold Fleet Ferry ♿

Baker Beach (3, B2)
Along the ocean side of the peninsula, this is the most picturesque of the city's beaches, with craggy rocks backed up against cliffs and the silent span of the Golden Gate Bridge. Swimming is not advisable.
☎ 561-4323 ✉ western end of the Presidio, Lincoln Ave to Bowley St
$ free 🕓 sunrise-sunset
🚌 28 ♿ no

Buena Vista Park (6, A6)
Enjoy stunning views of the city from this steep wooded hill separating the Castro from the Haight. Sometimes

used as an open-air playground for anonymous gay sex, the park is more sedate in the daytime.
☎ 831-2700
✉ Buena Vista Way off Haight & Baker Sts
$ free 🕓 sunrise-sunset
🚌 6, 7, 43, 71 ♿ no

Corona Heights (4, A2)
Overlooking the Castro between 15th and 16th Sts, this rugged little peak has a few trails and affords some really spectacular views. There's a playground, but the main reason to bring the kids here is the Randall Museum (p40).
☎ 831-2700 ✉ south of Buena Vista Park on Museum Way $ free
🕓 sunrise-sunset
🚌 37 ♿ no

Whale Watching
Gray whales pass the Bay Area on their way from the Bering Sea feeding grounds to the Baja California breeding grounds. You can see this majestic migration aboard one of the Oceanic Society Expeditions cruises (☎ 474-3385; www.oceanicsociety .org; $63/61 children 10 and older only; wheelchair accessible) that run January to May.

Mission Dolores Park offers a place to relax, to see and be seen - all in the middle of the city

Fort Funston (3, A6) A former military reserve that retains almost-wild nature right inside city limits. Rising from low dunes in the north to 200ft-high cliffs in the south, this was a coastal battery during WWII and a Nike missile base during the Cold War.
☎ 556-8371
✉ Great Hwy $ free
☾ 6am-9pm 🚌 Sloat Blvd to Great Hwy, left on Great Hwy ♿ limited

Marina Green (6, A1) The front lawn of the city overlooks all the stars of the bay. A favorite space for exercising.
☎ 831-2700 ✉ Marina Blvd from Webster to Scott Sts $ free ☾ sunrise-sunset 🚌 22 ♿

McKinley Park (3, E4) There are two crooked streets in the city – the block of Lombard from Hyde down to Leavenworth, which is filled with cars throughout the summer, and the stretch of Vermont from 20th to 22nd Sts, which is usually

empty. Come for the view of the Mission District and Twin Peaks, and for the ride.
☎ 831-2700
✉ Vermont & 20th Sts
$ free ☾ sunrise-sunset 🚌 53 🚌 16th St to Kansas St, right on 20th St to Vermont ♿

Mission Dolores Park (4, B2) A microcosm of the city in four blocks, this park has a playground and soccer pitch for the Mission Latinos, sunbathing for the gay boys from the Castro, tennis courts and picture postcard views for everybody.
☎ 831-2700
✉ bounded by 18th, Dolores, 20th & Church Sts
$ free ☾ sunrise-sunset 🚌 J line, 33 ♿

Ocean Beach (2, A3) On those rare sunny days, 4-mile-long Ocean Beach is a southern California beach scene with hard bodies and acrobatic surfers. Mostly, though, it is blanketed with fog and is a study in grays.
☎ 831-2700 ✉ bounded by Balboa Ave, Great Hwy

& Sloat Blvd $ free
☾ sunrise-sunset
🚌 N line, 5, 18, 23, 38, 48, 71 ♿

Portsmouth Square (5, C4) This is the only open space in Chinatown, and everyone takes advantage of it. See tai chi in the morning, kids playing in the afternoon and old men sitting around telling stories all day.
☎ 831-2700 ✉ Kearny St btwn Clay & Washington Sts $ free
☾ sunrise-sunset
Ⓜ Montgomery St
🚌 1, 15, 45 ♿

Union Square (5, B5) Named for the 1860s pro-union rallies, Union Square is the green heart of the city's shopping district. In the center of the park, Victory monument commemorates Admiral Dewey's success at Manila Bay in 1898.
☎ 831-2700
✉ bounded by Geary, Stockton, Powell & Post Sts
$ free ☾ sunrise-sunset Ⓜ Powell St

QUIRKY SAN FRANCISCO

AsiaSF (5, B8) Any restaurant can feature gender illusionist waitresses. Some can even feature gender illusionist dance routines. Only AsiaSF has the waitresses serving fusion food so good you don't notice their outfits. Reservations necessary.
☎ 255-2742 ▢ www .asiasf.com ✉ 201 9th St 💲 main meals $15 🕑 6-10pm Sun-Thu, 5-10pm Fri & Sat 🚌 12, 14, 19, 26 ♿

Bay to Breakers This may be the only serious foot race in the world with prizes for best costume. Athletes in every state of dress and undress make the 7½ mile run (or walk) from the Embarcadero to Ocean Beach. It's a classic San Francisco cross between a marathon and Mardi Gras.
▢ www.baytobreakers .com 💲 free to spectate 🕑 8am 3rd Sun in May ♿

Beach Blanket Babylon (5, B3) More than 30 years ago a revue about life in San Francisco opened at the Club Fugazi, featuring costumes and headdresses that redefined camp. Creator Steve Silver has passed to the big wardrobe department in the sky, but Beach Blanket goes on with lots of laughs and a memorable night. The show is for those aged 21 and over.
☎ 421-4222 ▢ www .beachblanketbabylon.com ✉ 678 Green St 💲 $25-75 🕑 8pm Wed & Thu, 7pm & 10pm Fri & Sat, 3pm & 7pm Sun 🚌 15, 30, 41, 45 ♿

Camera Obscura (2, A1) Beside the Cliff House, this Victorian-era amusement projects the outside ocean view onto a parabolic screen inside the building. This is one of the few remaining camera obscuras still left.
☎ 750-0415 ✉ 1096 Point Lobos Ave 🕑 9am-5pm 🚌 1, 2, 18, 38 ♿

Good Vibrations (4, C2) A visit to this sex toy shop is about as scandalous as going to the corner store to pick up a quart of milk. Good Vibrations is a women-owned collective with a mission – to provide an open and clean environment for positive sexual advancement.
☎ 522-5460 ▢ www.goodvibes.com ✉ 603 Valencia St 🕑 11am-7pm Sun-Wed, 11am-8pm Thu-Sat Ⓜ 16th St 🚌 14, 26, 33 ♿

Hang Gliders (3, A6) It's not your typical urban spectator sport, but every afternoon when the wind is up you can see hang gliders soaring above the ocean at Fort Funston. If you've never seen someone jump off a cliff right in front of you, this is your chance.
✉ Fort Funston 💲 free 🕑 sunrise-sunset (afternoons are best) 🚌 18, 23 🚗 Skyline Dr south from Sloat Blvd toward Daly City; turn right at Fort Funston sign and follow access road to the right to the parking lot at the edge of the cliffs ♿ limited

The cliffs at Fort Funston are a hang gliders' paradise

Mexican Bus (5, D6) Take a classic school bus, paint it like a pickup from Oaxaca, wire it for sound, and you have a Latin nightclub on wheels. Weekend tours take in three salsa clubs in the city with a fiesta en route. ☎ 546-3747, reservations required 🖥 www.mexicanbus.com ✉ pickup at Chevy's restaurant, 201 3rd St 💲 $38, no credit cards 🕑 dance club tour 9:30pm Fri & Sat 🚇 Montgomery St 🚌 15, 30, 45 to Chevy's ♿ no

Paxton Gate (4, C2)
Welcome to a macabre world of mounted tarantula, dead butterflies and stuffed mice dressed up in Elizabethan costumes. Artistic, disturbed and oddly alluring, the store's eclectic mix of orchids, garden gear and worthless knickknacks will encourage impulse buying. ☎ 824-1872 🖥 www.paxton-gate.com ✉ 824 Valencia St 💲 free 🕑 noon-7pm 🚇 16th St 🚌 26, 33 ♿

> **Critical Mass**
> The button-down life of **Justin Herman Plaza** (5, D4; Market St at the Embarcadero) turns into 'civilized anarchy' on the last Friday of every month. Known as Critical Mass, the event lacks formal leadership but retains one goal – to ride bicycles through the city streets. After a large enough crowd collects, the bikers set off en masse, tying up evening rush hour traffic. Showdowns between drivers and bikers are common, but most people come for the animal urges of running with a pack.

SAN FRANCISCO FOR CHILDREN

Aquarium of the Bay (5, B1) Walk amid schools of fish through hundreds of feet of underwater tunnels for an 'in-depth' aquarium experience. Exhibits recreate the different environments of San Francisco Bay, complete with such residents as giant Pacific octopus and bat rays. Check the website for the animal feeding schedule. ☎ 623-5300 🖥 www.aquariumofthebay.com ✉ Pier 39, Fisherman's Wharf 💲 $13/6.50, child under 3 free, family $30 🕑 10am-6pm Mon-Fri & 10am-7pm Sat & Sun Sep-May, 9am-8pm daily Jun-Aug 🚌 Powell-Mason cable car, F line,10, 15 ♿

California Academy of Sciences (5, C6) Making science approachable, this research organization maintains an aquarium and natural history exhibits that have temporarily relocated to South of Market while its Golden Gate Park facility is transformed into a 'green' building, with a living roof of native species. The Golden Gate Park site is closed until 2008. ☎ 750-7145 🖥 www.calacademy.org ✉ 875 Howard St 💲 $7/4.50/2, free 1st Wed of month, part of CityPass 🕑 10am-5pm 🚇 Powell St 🚌 any Market St bus, 14, 26, 27, 30 ♿

Exploratorium (3, C2)
One of the first science museums for kids, this is hands-on science with lots of excitement and overheard pleas from kids like, 'Mom, look at this,' 'Wow, let me do it.' Through cleverly designed games and demonstrations, kids learn about gravity, temperature and optical illusions. The bonus Tactile Dome (reservations required) is a sensory deprivation cave that is explored by feeling, sliding and crawling through it. ☎ 397-5673, Tactile Dome 561-0362 🖥 www.exploratorium.edu ✉ Palace of Fine Arts, 3601 Lygon St 💲 $12/9.50/8, Tactile Dome $15 (ages 7 & up) 🕑 10am-5pm Tue-Sun 🚌 28, 30 ♿

Fan Lot (5, E7) A mini-amusement park hiding in the outfield of SBC Park, features slides, a base race, and high kitsch stuff like a giant baseball glove, a giant Coca-Cola bottle and a miniature of SBC Park itself. ☎ 972-2000 ▯ www.sfgiants.com ✉ SBC Park, 24 Willie Mays Plaza $ free ☼ non-game days 11am-5pm Thu-Sun Sep-Dec & May, 11am-5pm daily Jun-Aug ▤ F, N line, 15, 30 ♿

Metreon (5, C6) Sony's ultramodern shopping mall, anchored by a multiplex cinema, blends commerce with the multimedia age. Where the Wild Things Are is a recreation of the famous picture book by Maurice Sendak ($6). Airtight Garage, a darkly lit grotto designed by graphic novelist Jean 'Moebius' Giraud, is a video arcade starring a virtual reality bowling alley. ☎ 800-638-7366 ▯ www.metreon.com ✉ 101 4th St $ admission free, fees apply for individual attractions ☼ 10am-10pm Sun-Thu, 10am-11pm Fri & Sat Ⓜ Powell St ▤ any Market St bus, 30, 45 ♿

Randall Museum (6, A6) Set in the heart of the city, the official children's museum has an animal orphanage and a small petting zoo, ideal for younger children. Other wild creatures, such as butterflies, sea lions and a mouse, dot the grounds as

Step into the future at the Metreon shopping mall

granite sculptures crafted by Beniamino Bufano. ☎ 554-9600 ▯ www.randallmuseum.org ✉ 199 Museum Way $ free ☼ 10am-5pm Tue-Sat ▤ 37 ♿

San Francisco Zoo (3, A5) With huge improvements in the works, the San Francisco Zoo is starting to emerge as a better attraction than in years past. A new lemur park, great ape exhibit, and African savanna are set to join the existing petting zoo. ☎ 753-7080 ▯ www.sfzoo.org ✉ 1 Zoo Rd

$ $10/7/4 ☼ 10am-5pm ▤ L line, 18, 23, 29 ▤ Sloat Blvd west to Zoo Rd ♿

Zeum (5, C6) This is a workshop for children to explore the technological arts, like animation, video production and digital design. Dedicated Zeum users suggest building a story board before your arrival and then using the production studio and animation lab to bring the story to life. There is also an exciting winding playground of ramps and slides, and technology exhibits. ☎ 777-2800 ▯ www.zeum.org ✉ 4th & Howard Sts $ $7/6/5 ☼ 11am-5pm Wed-Sun Sep-May, 11am-5pm Tue-Sun Jun-Aug Ⓜ Powell St ▤ 12, 14, 30, 45 ♿

Babysitting
Most good-size hotels have babysitting services, often provided by staff members who want to make a little money on the side. If yours does not, call **American ChildCare Service** (☎ 285-2300; www.american childcare.com; per hr $16.50, 4hr min).

Out & About

WALKING & BIKING TOURS
Bay to Bridge

Riding bikes across the Golden Gate Bridge is *more* 'San Francisco' than sourdough and cable cars. Start at **Blazing Saddles** (**1**; ☎ 202-8888; 1095 Columbus Ave, North Beach) to rent a bicycle and head north on Columbus, left on Beach St to the **Maritime Museum** (**2**; p30) and through Fort Mason Park. Turn right on Marina Blvd to **Fort Mason Center** (**3**; p30) and pick up lunch at **Greens** (p75). Continue along Marina Green until a right turn bisects the two boat marinas. At the end is **Wave Organ** (**4**; p33), a musical sculpture. Across Marina Blvd is the **Exploratorium** (p39) and further down Baker St is the **Palace of Fine Arts** (**5**; p28). Alternatively you can take the Golden Gate Promenade, a foot-and-bike path that skirts **Crissy Field** (**6**) to **Fort Point** (**7**; p21). Backtrack to Long Ave and hang a sharp right up steep Lincoln St to the mouth of the **Golden Gate Bridge** (**8**; p16). Follow the signs for bike traffic to cross the bridge.

Wander the passages at Fort Point

On the opposite side, take the first exit (Sausalito Lateral). You can lock up your bike here for a hike in the **Marin Headlands** (**9**; p47) or follow the road underneath the highway to **Sausalito** (**10**). Don't worry, it is all downhill from here. At the bottom catch the ferry back to Pier 41 at Fisherman's Wharf.

distance 8 miles
duration 2-4 hrs
▶ **start** cnr Columbus Ave & Francisco St;
🚋 Powell-Mason cable car
◉ **end**
🚢 Blue & Gold ferry (☎ 773-1188; www.blueandgoldfleet.com; ☀ 2 afternoon departures from Sausalito Mon-Fri, 3 afternoon departures Sat & Sun)

Mission Public Art

The Mission is an open-air gallery of raw creativity packaged as sanctioned and guerrilla art. Start at 16th and Mission Sts and go half a block east to the murals in **Redstone Building** (**1**; 2948 16th St). Backtrack to Valencia St and head south to **Clarion** and **Sycamore Alleys** (**2**). (Don't walk all the way down odoriferous Clarion.) At 18th St, a right turn will lead to the **Women's Building** (**3**; p33) mural and a left turn will lead to the **Generator Mural** (**4**; p32). Return to Valencia, an urban forest of covert street art that requires a birder's eye. Created by graphic artists with graffiti attitudes, posters, stencils and stickers claim the 'negative spaces' (sidewalks, lamp posts) and poke fun at pop culture and politics. Near 887 Valencia St is a **stencil** (**5**) of TV icon Mr T. The door of **Aquarius Records** (**6**; p57) is a hot spot for sticker art; look for ones by Pez. The **democracy wall** (**7**) near 1252 Valencia St is a legal poster wall dominated by activists, but with occasional appearances of chain mail pieces, like Shepard Fairey's *Andre the Giant*. Turn left at 24th St, and continue to Harrison St if you are interested in the **Precita Eyes Mural Center's** (**8**; p49) afternoon tour of Balmy Alley murals. Or you could wrap up at Mission St and grab a bite at **La Taquería** (**9**; p71).

Politics and art collide in the Mission

Tonantsin Renace © 1998 by Colette Crutcher

distance 1½ miles
duration 1hr plus 2½hr guided tour
▶ **start** cnr 16th & Mission Sts;
Ⓜ 16th St
◉ **end** 24th & Mission;
Ⓜ 24th St

Hippie Haight

Maybe you were there then, maybe you wish you were. Well, now you can pretend. Exit the bus at the corner of Haight and Baker St, next to the **Spencer House** (**1**), a stately Victorian at 1080 Haight St. Across the street is **Buena Vista Park** (**2**; p36) aptly named for its views. Turn right at Lyon St. The **building** (**3**) at 112 Lyon St is where Janis Joplin lived in 1967; she was kicked out for the benign infraction of having a dog. Backtrack to Haight St, heading west to the famous **Haight & Ashbury St corner** (**4**; p17), which was the geographic nucleus of the 1960s hippie scene. Turn left and continue until you reach 710 Ashbury St, a well-polished **Victorian** (**5**) that once housed the Grateful Dead. In 1967 the police raided the house and

Mourning the death of Jerry Garcia

found more groupies than pot and only two band members. Backtrack to Haight St and head to the Clayton St corner. The **Haight-Ashbury Free Clinic** (**6**) offers free medical care and is an enduring legacy of the neighborhood's 1960s experiment with freedom from capitalism and indulgence in drugs; the clinic was founded to treat overdoses. Finish the walk in Golden Gate Park at **Hippie Hill** (**7**), where an informal homage to the 1960s is held every weekend in the jam session drum circle.

A street performer on Haight St

distance 1½ miles
duration 1 hr
▶ start cnr Haight & Baker St;
🚌 6, 7, 71
⬤ end Golden Gate Park;
🚌 33

Russian Hill High

Up for some urban hiking and killer views? Bring water and a camera for this scenic tour. Start at Vallejo and Mason Sts and head west, toward the dead-end street. A stairway scales the cliff through **Ina Coolbrith Park (1)**, filled with wildflowers and a plateau where morning tai chi practitioners bless the silent city. Continue to the second set of stairs; now you've reached the top and a view of the Bay Bridge and Transamerica Pyramid. Follow gravity toward Jones St; turn right for a view of Alcatraz. The hill here is so steep that cars have to park perpendicular to the curb to prevent runaways. To your right is **MacCondray Lane (2)**, the inspiration for Babary Lane in Armistead Maupin's *Tales of the City*. Backtrack to Green St, and turn right. At 1067 Green St is **Feusier Octagon House (3)**, one of two remaining eight-sided houses in the

The eight-sided Feusier Octagon House

city. Continue to Hyde St and take a right. At the corner of Union St is the original Swenson's **ice-cream parlor (4)**. Once you have a cone in hand, continue north to **Lombard St (5**; p27), the world's crookedest street. Follow the switchbacks to Jones St, where a left will deliver you to the Diego Rivera mural at the **San Francisco Art Institute (6**; p34).

Lombard St, the world's crookedest street

distance 1 mile
duration 1 hr
▶ **start** cnr Vallejo & Mason Sts;
🚃 Powell-Mason cable car
● **end** Jones & Chestnut St;
🚃 Powell-Mason cable car

DAY TRIPS
Berkeley & Oakland (7)

Defining the far left, Berkeley has mellowed since the 1960s when students at the University of California at Berkeley clashed with the administration over free speech and withdrawal from Vietnam. Since then it has been busy instead amassing Nobel Prizes (18 have been awarded to UC Berkeley professors) and inventing a haute cuisine revolution. (Alice Waters and her Berkeley restaurant, Chez Panisse, are credited for the local, seasonal food component of California cuisine.)

The town's daily activities revolve around the UC Berkeley campus (called 'Cal' by its elite graduates). Besides sneering at students who don't look like geniuses, you can visit the **Berkeley Art Museum** (7, C1; BAM; ☎ 510-642-0808, www.bampfa.berkeley.edu; 2626 Bancroft Way, Berkeley; $8/5; ☺ 11am-5pm Wed-Sun, to 7pm Thu; BART Downtown Berkeley), showing everything from ancient Chinese paintings to modern sculpture. In the center of campus, the **Campanile** is a 307ft spire with 61 bells, ranging in size from a cereal bowl to a Volkswagen, with voices to match. Climbing up into the hills to the **Botanical Gardens** (☎ 510-643-2755; 200 Centennial Drive; $3/2/1; ☺ 9am-5pm, extended hours in summer; best reached by car) is a quick flirtation with wild California.

Next door is a mirror opposite image – brawny Oakland. The fourth largest port in the US and home of the infamous Raiders football team, Oakland is one of the most ethnically diverse cities in the country, but is too reserved to boast over it. Its major drawcard is the **Oakland Museum of California** (7, C6; ☎ 510-238-2200; www.museumca.org; 1000 Oak St; $8/5, free 2nd Sun of month; ☺ 10am-5pm Wed-Sat, noon-5pm Sun, to 9pm 1st Fri of month; BART Lake Merritt), focusing on California's cultural and natural history. Jack London's waterfront has been converted into a cheesy outdoor mall, redeemed solely by **Heinhold's First & Last Chance Saloon** (7, B6; ☎ 510-839-6761; 56 Jack London Square, Oakland; ☺ noon-midnight; BART 12th St), a crusty dive with an uneven floor caused by an earthquake or two. Oakland was also the birthplace and battleground of the Black Panther Party, a 1960s armed revolutionary group. A former member now hosts tours of the Panther's controversial history.

INFORMATION
Berkeley 10 miles, Oakland 9 miles east of San Francisco

🚗 Berkeley: I-80 across Bay Bridge to University Ave exit; east on University to Shattuck Ave & Oxford St
Oakland: I-80 across Bay Bridge, to 580 east, to 980 west, to downtown Oakland

ⓘ Legacy of the Panthers Tour (☎ 510-986-0660; www.blackpanthertours.com; $25)

✗ Café at Chez Panisse (p78)

The San Francisco skyline from Berkeley

Santa Cruz to Big Sur (1, B3)

The supermodel of coastlines, the California coast stretches south through leggy blonde beaches, precipitous cliffs and crashing waves that form a misty halo upon the shore. A typical California beach town, **Santa Cruz** is littered with itty-bitty bikinis, surfers and an old-fashioned **boardwalk** (☎ 831-426-7433; 400 Beach St, Santa Cruz; rides $1-4; ☽ 10am-6pm Jun-Sep) with rickety wooden rollercoasters, amusement rides and lots of junk food. Big and not-so-big kids can go on a serious sugar and adrenaline buzz with Halloween-style abandon. If you missed Fisherman's Wharf in San Francisco, dip south to the **Monterey Bay Aquarium** (☎ 831-648-4888; 886 Cannery Row, Monterey; $18/15/9; ☽ 10am-6pm). Sadly the surrounding town that John Steinbeck described so eloquently in *Cannery Row* is now a tacky tourist trap.

> ## INFORMATION
>
> *Santa Cruz 60 miles, Monterey 88 miles, Carmel 90 miles , Big Sur 113 miles south of San Francisco*
>
> 🚗 I-80 south to I-280, to Hwy 17 to Santa Cruz, Hwy 1 to Monterey, 17-Mile Drive (toll $8) to Carmel & Big Sur; return via Hwy 101
>
> ✗ Nepenthe (☎ 831-667-2345; Hwy 1, Big Sur; ☽ 11:30am-10pm)

If you don't have kids in tow, skip Monterey and follow the coastal roads of Hwy 1 and 17-Mile Dr through some breathtaking scenery and serious bank accounts to reach the hamlet of **Carmel**, formerly governed by actor Clint Eastwood. Reclusive Clint rarely receives strangers, but the seal pups at **Point Lobos State Reserve** (☎ 831-624-4909; Hwy 1, 3 miles south of Carmel; $6; ☽ 9am-7pm) are eager for paparazzi. Come early to avoid a wait.

Quite possibly the most beautiful piece of the planet, **Big Sur** is a long, scenic drive through wild and wondrous scenery protected by a series of state parks. With its arched sea caves and secluded cove, **Pfeiffer State Park** (☎ 800-444-7274; Hwy 1, Big Sur; $5 day use; ☽ sunrise-sunset) is Big Sur's most-photographed feature. To reach the beach road, go half a mile past the ranger station and look for a 'Vehicles over 20ft not recommended' sign marking the abrupt right turn. Consider staying overnight at **Deetjen's Big Sur Inn** (☎ 831-667-2377; www.deetjens.com; 48865 Hwy 1, Big Sur; $110-180) if you need more time to explore.

Awe-inspiring views of the coast along Highway 1, an easy day trip from the city

Mt Tamalpais & Marin Headlands (1, B2)

The rugged hills of the Marin Headlands lie north of the city and provide an easy escape into nature, as well as some striking views of the city and the Golden Gate Bridge. A steep road follows the exterior spine of the Marin Headlands exposing stacks of creased and wrinkled bedrock. As the road reaches the ocean, it dips like a rollercoaster toward the icy waters below. In spring, the hiking trails that criss-cross the headlands are covered with the golden cups of California poppies and purple lupine tassels.

Sitting on a meagre spit of land, **Point Bonita Lighthouse** is tethered to the mainland by a suspension bridge. To one side is the bay and the other is ocean, and both seem furious that the lighthouse hasn't tumbled from its pedestal.

The Bay Area's mountain deity is **Mt Tamalpais** (Mt Tam), standing a modest 2500ft high as the centerpiece of a collection of public parks that cover the coastline from the Golden Gate Bridge north to Tomales Bay. Mt Tam has 50 miles of hiking and biking trails that switchback through woods on the mountain's flank into meadows with views of the Golden Gate Bridge and the ocean. Even when the city is enshrouded in fog, Mt Tam usually peeks above into a pocket of sunshine. These steep trails gave birth to the rudimentary mountain bikes outfitted by daredevil locals speeding down these hills.

INFORMATION

Mt Tamalpais 10 miles, Marin Headlands 5 miles north of San Francisco

- 🚗 US 101 north across the Golden Gate Bridge to Marin Headlands (Alexander Ave exit); to Conselman Rd to Point Bonita Lighthouse parking lot; follow Bunker Rd to visitor center and to return to US 101; take Hwy 1 exit (Stinson Beach) and follow signs to Mt Tam
- ℹ️ Marin Headlands Visitor Center (☎ 415-331-1540; Fort Barry, Bldg 948; 🕑 9:30am-4:30pm) Mt Tamalpais State Park (☎ 415-388-2070; 801 Panoramic Hwy; parking $2; 🕑 sunrise-sunset)
- ✕ Mountain Home Inn (☎ 381-9000; 810 Panoramic Hwy, Mill Valley)

Grab your camera and climb Mt Tam for the best views of San Francisco

Napa & Sonoma Valleys (1, B2)

The birthplace of California's wine industry, Napa's long, slender valley combines the big sky wilderness of the American West with the tamed fertility of continental Europe. A monotonous expanse of captive grape vines fills the valley floor, lined on either side by swollen ridges wearing beards of dusty pines and scraggly brush. Thanks to the rich volcanic soil dumped by now-extinct Mt St Helena, grapes have thrived here since the 1850s.

INFORMATION

140 miles north of San Francisco

- I-80 east across the Bay Bridge to Hwy 29 exit; take Hwy 29 north to Napa Valley; Hwy 12 north to Sonoma Valley
- French Laundry (p78)

Shifting from consumption to appreciation, the Napa Valley wine makers started emulating European sophistication in the 1970s, and the region broke free of imitation at the famous 1976 French blind tasting, where two California wines (Stag's Leap 1973 cabernet sauvignon and Chateau Montelena's 1973 chardonnay) outscored French Bordeaux. Most of the famous wineries, situated along St Helena Hwy and Silverado Trail, feel like commercial behemoths with $10 wine tastings, pushy sales staff and crowded tasting rooms. More intimate and enjoyable are the smaller, family owned vineyards.

Petite **White Rock Vineyards** (☎ 707-257-7922; www.whiterockvineyards.com; 1115 Loma Vista Dr, Napa; by appointment) produces a complex claret (a combination of cabernet, merlot and petite verdot grapes) and a crisp chardonnay. Larger but still homey, **Havens** (☎ 707-261-2000; www.havenswine.com; 2055 Hoffman Lane, Napa; by appointment) entertains its visitors with merlots and syrahs under an oak tree. The valley's best view, however, can be found at **Storybook Mountain Winery** (☎ 707-942-5310; www.storybookwines.com; 3835 Hwy 128, Calistoga; by appointment), which is known for its juicy, expressive zinfandels.

To the west of the Napa Valley is the quieter Sonoma, where you will find the **Jack London State Historic Park** (☎ 707-938-5216; 2400 London Ranch Rd, Glen Ellen; $5 parking; park 9am-5pm, historic house noon-4pm Sat & Sun), comprising his former ranch, a museum and homestead. If traveling between the Napa and Sonoma Valleys, follow one of the twisting roads that summits the dividing mountain range.

Cabernets and chardonnays, rolling hills and valleys, just a few hours from San Francisco

ORGANIZED TOURS

Blue & Gold Fleet (5, B1)
This company offers a one-hour tour that loops under the Golden Gate Bridge and around Alcatraz, as well as ferries to Alcatraz, Angel Island, Sausalito, Tiburon and Oakland, and bus tours of Muir Woods, Napa Valley and Yosemite.
☎ 773-1188 ▫ www.blueandgoldfleet.com ✉ Pier 41 & 39 $ $20/16/12 ☝ bay cruises 10am-4pm ♿

Passengers on a tour boat on San Francisco Bay

Cruisin' the Castro (4, A2)
Trevor Hailey's walking tour of the Castro covers the landmarks and the history of San Francisco's gay community, from the Twin Peaks Tavern to Harvey Milk's camera shop.
☎ 550-8110 ✉ meet at Harvey Milk Plaza, Castro & Market Sts $ $40, lunch incl ☝ 10am-2pm Tue-Sat ▣ K, L, M lines to Castro, F line, 24 ♿ no

Precita Eyes Mural Center (3, E4) Every weekend, Precita Eyes presents walking tours of the Mission murals with information on the process and history of muralism and an explanation of symbolism and stories depicted in each mural.

The informative tours are the best way to explore Balmy Alley (p32) as well as other murals in the neighborhood.
☎ 285-2287 ▫ www.precitaeyes.org ✉ 2981 24th St $ $10/5/2 ☝ tours depart at 11am & 1:30pm Sat & Sun ⓜ 24th St ▣ 9, 12, 27, 48 ♿

Heritage Tours (6, C3)
The Foundation for San Francisco's Architectural Heritage offers informative two-hour tours of Pacific Heights' mansions and some of the simpler houses.
☎ 441-3004 ▫ www.sfheritage.org ✉ meet at Haas-Lilienthal House, 2007 Franklin St $ $8/5 ☝ 12:30pm Sun ▣ 1, 12, 47, 49 ♿ no

Dashiell Hammett Tour (5, A7) You will find fact and fiction merge on this tour of Dashiell Hammett's San Francisco. Follow Sam Spade and other noir detectives, as well as Hammett's own gumshoe work with the Pinkerton Detective agency with trench coated Don Herron as your guide.
☎ 287-9540 ▫ www.donherron.com ✉ meet at the Main Library, 100 Larkin St $ $10 ☝ noon Sun, reservations not require ⓜ Civic Center ▣ any Market St bus ♿ no

San Francisco City Guides
Walking tours of different neighborhoods, including districts such as the Mission, North Beach, Pacific Heights and Japantown, are organized under the auspices of the San Francisco Public Library and staffed by a team of volunteers.
☎ 557-4266 ▫ www.sfcityguides.org $ free ☝ May-Oct, schedules vary ♿

Stairway to Heaven
When the hills are too steep for sidewalks, concrete stairs run zigzag patterns to the summit through backyards and public gardens. The book *Stairway Walks in San Francisco*, by Adah Bakalinsky, describes 27 self-guided tours through charming neighborhoods with fantastic vistas.

Shopping

Conspicuous consumption is antithetical to the San Francisco anti-style (that's why 'Marina' is a bad word in some circles). Instead of worshipping labels and trends, this is a city of pack rats – they collect old records, obscure books, antique windup toys and designer labels. The junk filled shopping carts of the homeless population is the most extreme example of a citywide fetish.

While big name department stores proliferate, even on the beloved antiestablishment corner of Haight and Ashbury Sts, the citizens take pride in finding quirky local shops run by worker collectives or former 20-something 'CEOs' from the dot.com days. And of course the city that put flowers in the flower children's hair continues to play dress up today. Everyone has a fashionable costume – an amalgam of Sam Spade and '80s punk or straight up drag queen that is too outlandish or funky to be called the pedestrian term 'fashion.'

SHOPPING AREAS

Union Square is the heart of the headliners – Neiman-Marcus, Sax and other darlings of New York City's Fifth Avenue. Newcomers, like Levis (a San Francisco native), Gap and Nike, disrupt the lingering elegance of white glove days with dance club temples filled with more gadgets than merchandise. The streets are always packed with an infectious shopping euphoria and an egalitarianism not found in the East Coast. The best lesson learned during the Gold Rush days is that the millionaires of today were the paupers of yesterday.

Deeper into the shopping culture are two juxtaposed boutique strips – urban preppy Union St and urban bohemian Haight St – that cleave the population into irreconcilable cliques. Old World sophistication and imported shoes fill Hayes Valley, where everyone hopes to some day gracefully retire. A nouveau money stream also flows down the Pacific Heights thoroughfare of Fillmore St.

Used record shops and bookstores tend to congregate in the bohemian neighborhoods of North Beach, the Haight and the Mission.

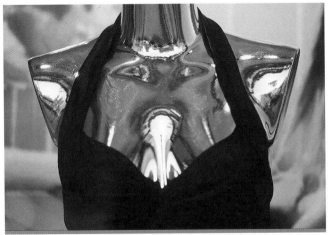

There's a fit for everyone in San Francisco's famed shopping districts

DEPARTMENT STORES & SHOPPING CENTERS

Macy's (5, C6) This is the West Coast flagship of the department store chain and the testing ground for new lines. Mainstream clothes and shoes are housed in a glass-enclosed building overlooking Union Square.
☎ 397-3333 ⌨ www.macys.com ✉ 170 O'Farrell Sts ☽ 10am-8pm Mon-Wed, 10am-9pm Thu-Sat, 11am-7pm Sun Ⓜ Powell St 🚌 2, 30, 38

Neiman-Marcus (5, C5) All the upper-crust designers and their couture compatriots are worshipped within these Beaux Art halls. Bring your checkbook or an American Express card, because it's one of the few places in the civilized world that does not take Visa or MasterCard.
☎ 362-3900 ⌨ www.neimanmarcus.com ✉ 150 Stockton St ☽ 10am-7pm Mon-Sat, noon-6pm Sun Ⓜ Powell St 🚌 2, 30, 38

Saks Fifth Avenue (5, C5) This blue blood New Yorker has made a fashionable adjustment to California living. The usual collection of classic designer women's clothes and cosmetics is nicely assembled in a small location on the sunny side of Union Square. The men's store is down the street at 220 Post St.
☎ 986-4300 ⌨ www.saksfifthavenue.com ✉ 384 Post St ☽ 10am-7pm Mon-Sat, to 8pm Thu, 11am-6pm Sun Ⓜ Powell St

San Francisco Shopping Centre (5, C6) This shopping mall in the middle of town turns conventional mall planning on its head. The boutiques (mainly branches of the chains you see in suburban malls) are on the first three floors, and the anchor – the Nordstrom department store – is on the top.
☎ 495-5656 ✉ 865 Market St ☽ hours vary Ⓜ Powell St 🚌 any Market St bus, 2, 30, 38

You'll find the chain stores in the San Francisco Shopping Centre

Levi's Original 501s

One of the greatest fashion revolutions since fig leaves, blue jeans are often credited to a young German immigrant named Levi Strauss. But the real kudos go to Jacob Davis, a San Franicisco tailor during the Gold Rush days. Davis modified the standard denim workpants with metal rivets to secure the corner pockets, rendering the pants indestructible. To protect his innovation, Davis needed a patent and a business partner. Meet Levi Strauss, a dry goods merchant and Davis' fabric supplier. Together they formed a now famous icon that adorns the backsides of millions of people around the world.

MARKETS

If northern California is in fact the France of the US, it's no surprise that San Francisco has a wealth of food and farmer's markets.

Berkeley Farmer's Market (7, B1 & C2)
More low key than the San Francisco versions, this biweekly open-air market offers produce (much of it certified organic), fresh bread, olive oils, cheeses, flowers and plants, plus prepared foods to tempt the hungry. If nothing else, it's a good place for people-watching (think aging hippies in hemp clothing).
☎ 510-548-3333
✉ Derby St & Martin Luther King Jr Dr (Tue), Center St & Martin Luther King Jr Dr (Sat)
Ⓜ Downtown Berkeley
🚌 AC Transit F bus from Transbay Terminal

Ferry Plaza Farmer's Market (5, E4) Encircling the recently renovated Ferry Building Marketplace (p77), this seasonal market attracts organic and boutique farmers, and the pocketbooks that can afford them. On weekends, much of the city meets here for grocery shopping, socializing and outdoor snacking beside the bay. If this doesn't make you want to move to California, you're incurable.
☎ 535-5650 🖥 www .ferryplazafarmersmarket .com ✉ One Ferry Building, Embarcadero & Market St 🕑 10am-2pm Tue, Thu & Sun, 8am-2pm Sat Ⓜ Embarcadero
🚌 F line

San Francisco Flower Mart (5, D8) With more than 80 fresh flower vendors, this wholesaler also opens its doors to the flower obsessed public. Orchids, roses, houseplants – come to browse, impulse buy or have breakfast at the Flower Mart Café. Weekends are busy.
☎ 392-7944 🖥 www .sfflmart.com
✉ 640 Brannan St
🕑 10am-3pm Mon-Sat
🚌 10, 47

United Nations Plaza Farmer's Market (5, B7)
This produce market for the proletariat was developed for the neighborhood's Southeast Asian immigrants. Live chickens, bulbous vegetables and petite women who scrutinize every bit of fruit are just some of the exotic sites that converge on the plaza, making it a distinctive experience from the coiffed Ferry Plaza Farmer's Market.
☎ 558-9455 ✉ UN Plaza, Market & 7th Sts
🕑 7am-5pm Wed & Sun
Ⓜ Civic Center
🚌 5, 6, 7, 66, 71

Farmer's markets bring fresh, locally grown produce to the city all year round

CLOTHING & JEWELRY

Amid the options, a few themes repeat: San Franciscans are not slaves to fashion, though they appreciate expressions of personal style. Clothing styles lean to the Italian and Asian when not indigenously American (the blue jean was invented here, after all).

Ambiance (2, F2) Stuffed with cute confections of retro inspirations, Ambiance elicits oohs and aahs from the dress wearing population. Victoriana jewelry, cocktail shifts and prom dresses that don't look like marshmallow outfits are delicately handled by an eagle eye and bony elbow crowd. There's another branch at 1864 Union St (6, B2; ☎ 923-9797).
☎ 552-5095 ⊠ 1458 Haight St ⏱ 10am-7pm Mon-Sat, 11am-7pm Sun ⊟ N line, 6, 7, 71

Billy Blue (5, C5) Here you can find high-powered suits and vibrant ties from Milan (and elsewhere in Italy), and American clothiers who speak or at least appreciate Italian. Find one-off designs that deliver European style with American comfort and a knowledgeable staff.
☎ 781-2111 ⏐ www .billyblue.com ⊠ 54 Geary St ⏱ 10am-6pm Mon-Sat ⓜ Montgomery or Powell St ⊟ 2, 3, 4

Buffalo Exchange (2, F2) In the thrifting hierarchy, Buffalo Exchange is the quiet girl next door. Mainstream numbers roll through for the T-shirt collectors and bargain basic hunters. Shoes, handbags and those 'I'm with the band' sunglasses are other good staples.
☎ 431-7737 ⏐ www .buffaloexchange.com ⊠ 1555 Haight St ⏱ 11am-7pm Mon-Thu, to 8pm Fri-Sun ⊟ N line, 6, 7, 71

Bulo (6, C5) If you happen to be looking for a special pair of Italians to match your luxury car, you'll find a fine selection of imported leather shoes, especially boots, here in the heart of Hayes Valley shoe paradise. The men's and women's stores eye each other off from opposite sides of the street.
☎ 225-4935 ⊠ 418 & 453 Hayes St ⏱ 11am-6:30pm Mon-Sat, noon-6pm Sun ⊟ 21

De Vera (5, C5) Maiden Lane, a former red light district, has come a long way. Now the ladies of the day and night can crown themselves with any of a vast array of gems, diamonds and gold.
☎ 788-0828 ⊠ 29 Maiden Lane ⏱ 10am-6pm Mon-Sat ⓜ Powell St ⊟ Powell-Hyde & Powell-Mason, 5, 30, 45

CLOTHING & SHOE SIZES

Women's Clothing

Aust/UK	8	10	12	14	16	18
Europe	36	38	40	42	44	46
Japan	5	7	9	11	13	15
USA	6	8	10	12	14	16

Women's Shoes

Aust/USA	5	6	7	8	9	10
Europe	35	36	37	38	39	40
France only	35	36	38	39	40	42
Japan	22	23	24	25	26	27
UK	3½	4½	5½	6½	7½	8½

Men's Clothing

Aust	92	96	100	104	108	112
Europe	46	48	50	52	54	56

Japan	S	M	M		L	
UK/USA	35	36	37	38	39	40

Men's Shirts (Collar Sizes)

Aust/Japan	38	39	40	41	42	43
Europe	38	39	40	41	42	43
UK/USA	15	15½	16	16½	17	17½

Men's Shoes

Aust/UK	7	8	9	10	11	12
Europe	41	42	43	44½	46	47
Japan	26	27	27.5	28	29	30
USA	7½	8½	9½	10½	11½	12½

Measurements approximate only; try before you buy.

HRM Boutique (4, C2)
There's nothing casual about the casual clothes for men and women here. Designed and sewn in-house, they have everything you like about Banana Republic without the worry that every third person on the street will be wearing it.
☎ 642-0841
💻 www.hrmclothing.com
✉ 924 Valencia St
🕑 noon-7pm
🚌 14, 26, 49

Leather Etc (5, B8) This might not be a surprise, but San Francisco has a loud and proud leather scene centered around South of Market. Buttless chaps, fetish fashion and PVC lingerie don't really qualify as office wear (maybe on casual Friday) but are prerequisites for the Folsom St Fair (p80).
☎ 864-7558
💻 www.leatheretc.com
✉ 1201 Folsom St
🕑 10am-8pm Mon-Sat, 11am-6pm Sun 🚌 12, 19

MAC (5, C5) With a 20-year reputation for spotting

trends, Modern Appealing Clothing delivers a city smart look for men, women and baby. Manifesto, John Bartlett, Paul Smith and Kenzo, and lesser names afford similar style and comfort.
☎ 837-0615
✉ 5 Claude Ln
🕑 11am-6pm Mon-Sat, noon-5pm Sun
Ⓜ Montgomery or Powell St 🚌 2, 3, 4, 15, 30

Mrs Dewson's Hats (6, B3)
Friendly Ruth Dewson (that's Mrs to you) operates the counter at her long-running hat store, which crowned Willie Brown (the impeccably dressed former mayor) with a namesake number. Many of her other creations are extravagant pieces best admired in church on Sunday.
☎ 346-1600 ✉ 2050 Fillmore St 🕑 11am-6pm Tue-Sat, noon-4pm Sun
🚌 1, 3, 22

Rabat (6, A2) With its flirty cocktail dresses in sassy colors and matching shoes to die for, Rabat

modernizes the fantastic 1940s, cuts loose with futuristic avant garde and somehow avoids all those trifling trends.
☎ 929-8868 ✉ 2080 Chestnut St 🕑 10:30am-6pm 🚌 22, 30

Rolo (4, A2) A homegrown chain for the sporty baby tee lovers, Rolo dips into a variety of fashion labels from Paul Smith, Miu-Miu and Comme des Garçons.
Rolo's Garage (5, B8; ☎ 861-2097; 1301 Howard St) is the factory outlet with lots of bargains.
☎ 431-4545
💻 www.rolo.com
✉ 2351 Market St
🕑 11am-8pm Mon-Sat, noon-7pm Sun 🚌 K, L, M lines to Castro, F line, 24

Shoe Biz (2, F2) Did you know Vans were back? Just one stop at Shoe Biz will tell you when to resurrect your banned footwear.
☎ 864-0990 💻 www.shoebizsf.com ✉ 1446 Haight St 🕑 11am-7pm Mon-Sat, noon-6pm Sun
🚌 6, 7, 33, 43, 71

Sunhee Moon (4, B2)
This place has classic thin-wale corduroys for foggy San Francisco days, Asian-influenced jackets and fitted slacks that are versatile day- and night- wear for sensible fashionistas. Many of Sunhee's designs are geared toward petites who have a hard time finding pants that fit.
☎ 355-1800 ✉ 3167 16th St 🕑 noon-6pm Mon-Fri, to 5pm Sat & Sun
Ⓜ 16th St 🚌 22

Vintage Vestments

Here at the end of the continental shelf, people and junk continually get a second chance at life – an end of the road resurrection. Used clothes, plastic flotsam and dinosaur cars are respectively recycled into alternative fashion, front yard dioramas or art cars. And the city's appreciation for this kind of creative kitsch rivals that of the self-conscious pinnacle defined by John Waters. A vintage coat older than its owner is more prized than the nouveau leather jackets that serve as urban passports in Los Angeles and New York. To amass a discarded empire, visit **Wasteland** (p55), **Thrift Town** (p55) and **Buffalo Exchange** (p53).

Wilkes Bashford houses five floors of the best of Italian, French and American designers

Thrift Town (4, C2) This massive two-story edifice is everything a hometown charity shop should be. A visitor will find more spectacle observing the frantic customers than browsing the dusty collections of used clothes, underwear (?), uniforms, housewares and furniture. But if you're a gag gift giver, there are bowling trophies.
☎ 861-1132 ⊠ 2101 Mission St ⏱ 9am-8pm Mon-Fri, 10am-7pm Sat, 11am-6pm Sun Ⓜ 16th St 🚌 14, 22, 49

Wasteland (2, F2) The catwalk of thrifting, Wasteland has the pick of the city's closets for label whores and fashion rebels. Every era is well represented and there's a great collection of hats, leather jackets and roller-sneakers to peruse.
☎ 863-3150 ⊠ 1660 Haight St ⏱ 11am-8pm 🚌 N line, 6, 7, 71

Wilkes Bashford (5, C5) An institution for more than 30 years, this store has five floors of the finest fashions for men and women. Surrender yourself and your credit cards to a salesperson and see where the best Italian, French and American designers take you.
☎ 986-4380 🖥 www .wilkesbashford.com ⊠ 375 Sutter St ⏱ 10am-6pm Mon-Sat, to 8pm Thu Ⓜ Powell St 🚌 2, 3, 4, 30

FOOD & DRINK

Bombay Bazaar (4, B2) Adding to the college campus atmosphere of Valencia St, Bombay Bazaar carries all the Indian necessities you could possibly need – spices, samosas, henna tattoos – to complement your recent ashram addiction. Bombay Bazaar's affiliated ice-cream shop scoops such exotic flavors as ginger, mango and fig.
☎ 621-1717 ⊠ 548-552 Valencia St ⏱ 10am-7pm Tue-Sat Ⓜ 16th St 🚌 22, 26

Ghirardelli Soda Fountain & Chocolate Shop (6, C1) Established in 1852, San Francisco–based Ghirardelli enjoys the longest chocolate making tradition in the US. Its flagship store is in an old chocolate factory and sells snacks, gifts and on-site delicacies, if you can't wait until you get home.
☎ 771-4903 🖥 www .ghirardelli.com ⊠ 900 North Point St ⏱ 9am-11pm Sun-Thu, to midnight Fri & Sat 🚌 Powell-Hyde cable car, 19, 30

Joseph Schmidt Confections (4, B2) Trained as a baker in Europe, Joseph Schmidt has since forsaken pastries for a solo chocolate career. Luscious and creative his ensemble includes truffles, mints and holiday-themed sculptures you'll have to taste to be convinced it is chocolate.
☎ 861-8682 🖥 www .jschmidtconfections.com ⊠ 3489 16th St ⏱ 10am-6:30pm Mon-Sat 🚌 J line, 22

Based in San Francisco since 1852, the Ghirardelli store is *the* place to satisfy your chocolate cravings

Kermit Lynch Wine Merchant (7, A1)

This may be an out of towner, but it's well worth the trip. Regarded as one of the best boutiques for hard-to-find European wines from Burgundy and Rhône, Kermit Lynch occupies a revered seat along Berkeley's gastronomic pantheon.
☎ 510-524-1524
✉ 1605 San Pablo Ave, Berkeley ☽ 11am-6pm Tue-Sat ⛟ east on I-80, over Bay Bridge to Gilman exit, east on Gilman to San Pablo, south on San Pablo to corner of Cedar

PlumpJack Wines (6, B2)

An uncommonly good wine shop, PlumpJack is fancy enough for Pacific Heights matrons and accessible enough for the rest of us. There's a wide selection and a staff who don't mind helping you decide.
☎ 346-9870
✉ 3201 Fillmore St
☽ 11am-8pm Mon-Sat, to 6pm Sun ⛟ 22

Wine Club (5, C7)

This warehouse near the Hall of Justice looks more like a machine shop than a clearinghouse for fine beverages. But the doors are open for the grape lovers; come and educate your palate with wines on offer for tasting (you must be 21 though).
☎ 512-9086
🖥 www.thewineclub.com
✉ 953 Harrison St
☽ 9am-7pm Mon-Sat, 11am-6pm Sun ⛟ 27, 47

How to Speak Panhandler

San Francisco is an empathetic place that tolerates and even encourages panhandling. Regardless of personal politics, everyone abides by a strict etiquette that can best be described as speaking in code. Here is a typical exchange (with translation) between a panhandler and a passing person.

Panhandler: 'Spare some change?'
(Translation = 'Hi how are you?')
Passing Person: 'Sorry.'
(Translation = 'I'm good and you?')
Panhandler: 'Thanks anyway' or 'Have a nice day.'
(Translation = self-explanatory)

Both actors continue with their day's pursuits having politely greased the city's social mechanism. If a passing person fails to acknowledge the opening question, great offense is caused and often a panhandler will discipline them harshly.

BOOKS & MUSIC

A Clean Well Lighted Place for Books (5, A7)

It would be gauche to shop at Borders in this pro-local town. Instead, San Franciscans visit this aptly named bookstore for general titles and independent solidarity. There is also a full literary calendar and a staff that actually knows and reads books.

☎ 441-6670 ⌨ www
.bookstore.com ✉ Opera
Plaza, 601 Van Ness Ave
🕓 10am-11pm Mon-Sat,
10am-9pm Sun
🚇 J, K, L, M, N lines to
Van Ness, F line, 47, 49

A Different Light (4, A2)

This is the premiere gay and lesbian bookstore, featuring fiction and nonfiction, travel literature, poetry, cards and photographs since 1979. Check its calendar for literary events.

☎ 431-0891 ⌨ www
.adlbooks.com ✉ 489
Castro St 🕓 10am-11pm
🚇 K, L, M lines, 24, 33

Amoeba Records (2, E2)

One of the best and biggest used record stores in the world (no joke), Amoeba sprawls over every inch of this former bowling alley with over 750,000 pieces of music (tapes, CDs, LPs) and every imaginable genre. Regulars are obsessive about searching the stacks at Amoeba – showing up before the doors open and following the employees out at the end of the day.

☎ 831-1200
⌨ www.amoebamusic
.com ✉ 1855 Haight St

🕓 10:30am-10pm
Mon-Sat, 11am-9pm Sun
🚇 N line, 6, 7, 33, 71

Aquarius Records (4, C3)

Everything you need to infuse your aging classic rock collection with the 21st century. Mainly CDs with a few well-thumbed LPs, Aquarius is a selective repository for ambient sounds, world music, hip-hop and indie rock.

☎ 647-2272 ⌨ www
.aquariusrecords.org
✉ 1055 Valencia St
🕓 10am-9pm Mon-Wed,
10am-10pm Thu-Sun
Ⓜ 24th St 🚇 14, 26

Bound Together Bookstore (2, F2)

Carrying the torch since 1976 for the simmering anarchist movement, this subdued collective carries AK Press, poetry books, and some magic and queer titles. Obsessed with telling it like it is, the Bay Area is a prolific zine producer, including *Maximum Rock-NRoll*, *Cometbus* and others available here.

☎ 431-8355 ⌨ www
.boundtogether.org
✉ 1369 Haight St
🕓 11am-7:30pm
🚇 N line, 6, 7, 71

City Lights Bookstore (5, C3)

More than just a bookstore, this is a literary legend. Founded by poet Lawrence Ferlinghetti, City Lights was the country's first paperback bookstore and the publisher of Allen Ginsberg's *Howl* in 1956. (The poem was later banned for obscenity, Ginsberg was charged and the work was subsequently immortalized.) Today Beat poetry occupies the 2nd floor.

☎ 362-8193
⌨ www.citylights.com
✉ 261 Columbus Ave
🕓 10am-midnight
🚇 15, 30, 41, 45

Inside the legendary City Lights Bookstore

Discolandia (3, E4) A fixture of time warped 24th St, this CD and tape store shuffles through merengue and salsa to the accordion strains of Tejano.
☎ 826-9446 ✉ 2964 24th St 🕓 11:30am-6:30pm Mon-Sat, noon-4pm Sun 🚌 9, 48

Green Apple Books (2, D1) Bespeckled bookphiles come to this local legend to pan for golden titles amid the stacks of used and new books. There are claustrophobic spaces, creaking wooden floors and twitchy patrons – all that's missing from this quintessential scene is a lazy cat. Staff write-ups accompany recently reviewed favorites.
☎ 387-2272 🖥 www .greenapplebooks.com ✉ 506 Clement St 🕓 10am-10:30pm Sun-Thu, to 11:30pm Fri & Sat 🚌 1, 2, 38, 44

Jack's Record Cellar (6, B5) The collector's collection, Jack's is a dust-filled museum for the anemic, tweed-clad vinyl geeks. Eclectic and obscure 78s and LPs cover mainly country, bluegrass and jazz with a little rock and R&B as well.
☎ 431-3047 ✉ 254 Scott St 🕓 noon-7pm Wed-Sat 🚌 6, 22, 24, 71

Modern Times Bookstore (4, C2) Minority voices and progressive politics, along with the self-proclaimed 'best-looking' clerks in San Francisco are showcased at this collectively owned bookstore. There are also Spanish language and Chicano sections, and an extensive Latino history and culture collection.
☎ 282-9246 🖥 www.mtbs.com ✉ 888 Valencia St 🕓 10am-9pm Mon-Sat, 11am-6pm Sun 🚌 26, 33

Rooky Ricardo's Records (6, B5) Looking for soul and pop on bread plate–sized

Stories of San Francisco

Great wits, offbeat characters, no goods and gumshoes fill the literary depictions of San Francisco (see p109).

- *The Barbary Coast: An Informal History of the San Francisco Underworld,* by Herbert Asbury (the author of *Gangs of New York*), follows San Francisco's Wild West days.
- *You Can't Win,* by Jack Black, is an autobiography of an early-20th-century jack-of-all-nefarious-trades (cat burglar, stickup man, prison kingpin) that was a favorite of the Beats.
- *The Electric Kool-Aid Acid Test,* by Tom Wolfe, follows LSD guru Ken Kesey and his Merry Pranksters in their Day-Glo bus on their hallucinogenic trip.
- *The Maltese Falcon,* by Dashiell Hammett, is the classic hard-boiled crime story about San Francisco detective Sam Spade and his mix-up with one tough dame.

45s? Motown lives on in this simple storefront near a popular daytime corner in layabout Lower Haight.
☎ 864-7526 ⌨ www .rookyricardosrecords.com ✉ 448 Haight St ⊙ 1-6pm Mon-Fri, noon-6pm Sat & Sun 🚌 6, 22, 71

William K Stout Architectural Books
(5, C4) Building buffs and architecture aficionados will find lots to browse in this cramped space filled with adult-sized picture books. Architecture, design, how-tos and Bay Area themes are just a few choices; playing 'stump the clerk' is also a welcome game.
☎ 391-6757 ⌨ www.stoutbooks.com ✉ 804 Montgomery St ⊙ 10am-6:30pm Tue-Fri, to 5:30pm Sat 🚌 15, 30, 41, 45

FOR CHILDREN

If you're shopping *for* children, Laurel Heights (California St between Laurel and Spruce Sts) has the best selection of clothing boutiques. But if you're shopping *with* children, go straight to Chinatown's Grant Ave or Fisherman's Wharf.

Chinatown Kite Shop
(5, C4) Colorful and whimsical, this shop will make the expression 'go fly a kite' seem like a great idea. Fighting kites, parafoils, wind wheels and even kites shaped like helicopters will surely distract your children away from the Chinese throwing stars available at nearby vendors.
☎ 989-5182 ✉ 717 Grant Ave ⊙ 10am-9pm 🚋 Powell-Mason & Powell-Hyde cable cars, 1, 15

Dottie Doolittle (3, C2)
If Bergdorf Goodman department store had a children's department, this is what it would look like. There are colorful dresses for the princess in your life, as well as outfits for your little man.
☎ 563-3244 ✉ 3680 Sacramento St ⊙ 10am-6pm Mon-Sat, noon-5pm Sun 🚌 1, 43

Jeffrey's Toys (5, C6) This is a throwback to another era when toys came from places homier than Toys 'R' Us. Kid's comics, stuffed animals and collectors' toys seem to attract more parents than kids, proof that it is the adults messing up the playroom.
☎ 243-8697 ✉ 685 Market St ⊙ 9am-8pm Mon-Fri, 10am-8pm Sat, 11am-6pm Sun Ⓜ Montgomery St 🚌 5, 6, 7, 15, 30

Jonathan-Kaye Baby
(3, C2) Precious non-necessities for newborns and nurseries, from handmade booties to tiny rocking chairs and linens. A large selection of fashionable diaper bags will liberate you from the usual cutesy plastic numbers. There are two Jonathan-Kaye stores across the street from each other.
☎ 563-0773 ✉ 3548 & 3615 Sacramento St ⊙ 10am-6pm Mon-Sat, noon-5pm Sun 🚌 1

There are plenty of shopping options for those with kids

Kid's Only (2, F2) Baby tie-dyes or bumble bee rain jackets with matching galoshes might deter the littlest ones from demanding other Haight St paraphernalia. Do they really need another piercing or water pipe? Even if the kid's wardrobe is complete with hand-me-downs, stop in to browse Kid's Only's collection of books and puzzles.
☎ 552-5445 ✉ 1608 Haight St ☉ 10:30am-6:30pm Mon-Fri, 10am-6pm Sat, 11am-5pm Sun 🚊 N line, 6, 7, 71

Tuffy's Hopscotch (3, D2) Shoes take center stage at Tuffy's, from tiny versions of the big names to a fantastic selection of little girly-girl sandals (with strawberry and cherry motifs) that will make any fashion-conscious mother proud (and probably want a pair herself).
☎ 440-7599 ✉ 3307 Sacramento St ☉ 10am-6pm Mon-Sat, noon-5pm Sun 🚊 1, 43

Wee Scotty (6, B2) Lynne Gallagher creates these whimsical accents on-site with youthful input from her own daughter. Happy birthday piñata pants and neon shag jackets will complete the rock and roll fantasies of any rebellious tweener.
☎ 345-9200 ✉ 2266 Union St ☉ 11am-6pm 🚊 22, 41, 45

SPECIALTY STORES

Flax Art (6, C5) Called a 'candy store for the creative,' this family owned emporium stocks everything in the way of art supplies. One could spend hours dawdling over the selection of papers alone but for the siren call of the pens on their counters nearby.
☎ 552-2355 🖥 www .flaxart.com ✉ 1699 Market St ☉ 9:30am-6pm Mon-Sat, 11am-6pm Sun 🚊 J, K, L, M, N lines to Van Ness, 6, 7, 71

Chong Imports (5, C4) Grant Ave is packed with Chinatown-themed accessories that lose their entertainment value once you hit the airport. The neighborhood's best buys are the industrial strength chopping blocks and ceramic bowls sold at this shop for third world prices.
☎ 982-1432 🖥 www .chongimports.com ✉ 838 Grant Ave, enter from Walter Lum Pl across from Portsmouth Sq ☉ 10am-8pm Mon-Sat, noon-8pm Sun 🚊 California St cable car, 1, 30, 45

Clarion Music Center (5, C4) Traditional musical instruments from all over the world wait patiently to be played by knowledgeable hands. In order to shop for these coaxable singers, a browsing musician must massage the strings, pound the drums, and be prepared to give an impromptu concert to the musical spectators.
☎ 391-1317 🖥 www .clarionmusic.com ✉ 816 Sacramento St ☉ 11am-6pm Mon-Fri, 9am-5pm Sat 🚊 California St cable car, 1, 30, 45

George (6, B3) If your bundle of joy also coughs up fur balls, then George is the store for you. Catnip mouse toys made of knitted alpaca, for the feline aesthetes, and dog bone knick knacks are perfect birthday gifts for your four-legged child.
☎ 441-0564 ✉ 2411 California St ☉ 10am-6pm Mon-Sat, noon-6pm Sun 🚊 1, 22

Kiehl's (6, B3) An outpost of the historic New York pharmacy carries all of the high-end beauty products

The renovated Ferry Building Marketplace is a popular place to shop and eat on weekends

that have earned the company a cultish following. Don't forget that samples are gladly given, and lab-smocked 'consultants' are on hand for questions.
☎ 359-9260
🖳 www.kiehls.com
✉ 2360 Fillmore St
🕓 10am-7pm Mon-Sat, noon-6pm Sun 🚌 1, 22

Lombardi Sports (6, C3)
This locally owned sporting goods store has the right stuff for all the local sports (with the possible exception of surfing) and a staff that obviously goes outside to play.
☎ 771-0600 🖳 www.lombardisports.com
✉ 1600 Jackson St
🕓 10am-7pm Mon-Wed,

to 8pm Thu & Fri, to 6pm Sat & Sun 🚌 19, 47, 49

Nest (6, B3) Beautiful quilts, knitted baby wear and other home accessories – these are all the things you've envisioned making if only you had the time, skill and creativity. Yeah, give up the Martha Stewart fantasy and just pay for someone else's handiwork.
☎ 292-6199
✉ 2300 Fillmore St
🕓 10am-6pm 🚌 1, 22

Pipe Dreams (2, F2) This head shop has kept the peace pipe going since the '60s got rolling. Glass water pipes, incense and hippie paraphernalia are pawed

over by wide-eyed teenagers with visions of Cheech & Chong in their heads.
☎ 431-3553 ✉ 1376 Haight St 🕓 10am-7pm Mon-Sat, 11am-7pm Sun
🚌 6, 7, 33, 43

San Francisco Rock Poster Collectibles (5, B3)
Big Brother & the Holding Company, Grateful Dead, Jefferson Airplane, even Ma Rainey appeared in the bubbly lettering of the 1960s concert posters that are now collectors items in this grown-up's version of a head shop.
☎ 956-6749 ✉ 1851 Powell St 🕓 10am-6pm Tue-Sat 🚌 Powell-Mason cable car, 15, 39

Eating

Like a sophisticated shopper in the world's culinary market, San Francisco has selected its favorite aspects of French, Italian and Asian traditions to create an exciting cuisine suited to the bounty of land and sea. Left behind in the Old World are heavy butter and cream sauces designed for harsh winters. Enthusiastically adopted were olive oils, piquant spices and cooking techniques such as searing or blanching that complement the city's healthy ideals.

Innovation in cuisine has coincided with innovation in food production. Organic, locally grown, grass-fed – an environmental credo is professed on almost every menu. This progressive consciousness crosses over into boy band hysteria with the release of new boutique vegetables – rocket one year, mâche the next. It is hard to keep up.

Meal Costs

The pricing symbols used in this chapter indicate the cost for one main dish.

$	under $10
$$	$11-20
$$$	$21-28
$$$$	over $29

But people do keep up because San Franciscans love to have hobbies – from mountain biking to playing in a klezmar (Jewish) band. And with more restaurants per capita than any other US city, San Franciscans have a reputation too. Talking about restaurants ranks just above another favorite: real estate and rents (sex, drugs and rock and roll take a distant third).

All this talking will surely make you thirsty, especially for those famous California chardonnays and cabernets. In gourmet restaurants, sommeliers are pleasurable guides in matching food and wine. Local microbrews include piney Sierra Nevada and Anchor Steam. The city supposedly invented the martini and the Irish coffee, both of which taste deliciously genuine anywhere.

Californians are generous tippers. Most checks warrant a 20% tip on dinner and 15% on lunch and breakfast. No formal rules have evolved regarding the ubiquitous tip jars at coffee shops, but most pink-haired baristas insist that tipping equals good karma.

Now that you're all excited to eat fabulously, be warned that the most famous restaurants require advance reservations (call today). The reviews following note the particularly tricky ones. Also a statewide ban prohibits smoking in public buildings, including restaurants.

Innovative cuisine and passionate local palates keep the city's culinary traditions alive

THE CASTRO & UPPER MARKET

Anchor Oyster Bar (4, A2) $

Seafood

A family-owned raw bar, Anchor harks back to the time when the Castro was a working-class village. Oysters on the half shell, the regional dish of crab and shrimp Louie and spicy oyster shooters are served up to a steady stream of low-key locals too well-fed and content to cast the neighborhood's cruisey eye. ☎ 431-3990 ✉ 579 Castro St ☽ 11:30am-10pm ☒ K, L, M lines to Castro, 24 ♿ Ⓥ ♿

Blue (4, A2) $$

American

This grey-and-black sexy number passes as a 'what, this old thing?' stand-by among Castro's fashion-conscious denizens. Comfort food and diner stalwarts get an invigorating makeover – such as the tarragon kissed chicken pot pie – served with a side dish of pulse quickening ambience music. The sidewalk seats are coveted spots with the brunch brigade. ☎ 863-2583 ✉ 2337 Market St ☽ 11:30am-11pm ☒ K, L, M lines to Castro, 24 ♿ Ⓥ ♿

Café Flore (4, A2)

American

Like a backyard humming-bird feeder, this sunny café attracts a rotating cast of characters – from moody gay activists glued to thick political treatises to mommies saddled to SUV strollers. Great salads

Hearty breakfasts are just one of Café Flore's draws

and hearty breakfasts are nibbled and noshed behind a luscious green curtain of potted plants. ☎ 621-8579 ✉ 2298 Market St ☽ 7am-11pm ☒ K, L, M lines to Castro, F line, 24 ♿ Ⓥ ♿

Catch (4, A2) $$

Seafood

Amid the brick walls and blond wood is a big Swedish fireplace, a tinkling piano, and the bubble of conversation from birthday celebrations and armies of singles. Mussels with Pernod and seafood risotto are served in a little tub for two, and the grilled salmon is wild just like your date. ☎ 431-5000 ✉ 2362 Market St ☽ 5:30-10pm Mon-Fri, 11:30am-3pm Sat & Sun ☒ K, L, M lines to Castro, F line, 24 Ⓥ ♿

Chow (4, B1) $

American

Every town has one of these stand-in kitchens for when the cupboard is bare. Even the college pub atmosphere is tried and true. Being San Francisco, however, the usual fried anything is

replaced by organic garden pizzas and prawn salads. It can get busy though, so skip to other culinary adventures if there is a line. Other branch: **Park Chow** (2, D1; ☎ 665-9912; 1238 9th Ave, Sunset). ☎ 552-2469 ✉ 215 Church St ☽ 11am-11pm Sun-Thu, 10am-midnight Fri & Sat ☒ F, J lines, 22 ♿ Ⓥ ♿

Firewood Café (4, A2) $

Italian

Your food fantasies might be dashed when you follow a local's suggestion to this spiffy local chain. Firewood Café fizzles with mall-like decor but the menu dazzles with selections like wholesome roast chicken, wood-fired pizzas and monster salads. There are other branches at **Union Square** (5, J4; ☎ 788-3473; 3233 Geary St) and **Metreon** (5, C6; ☎ 369-6299; 101 4th St). ☎ 252-0999 ✉ 4248 18th St ☽ 11am-10:30pm Mon-Thu, to 11pm Fri & Sat, to 10pm Sun ☒ K, L, M lines to Castro, F line, 24, 33 ♿ ♿

CHINATOWN

Gold Mountain (5, C3) $$
Chinese

Sporting a 1980s Hong Kong chic, Gold Mountain is usually monopolized by Chinese families rather than ethno foodies. The gruff servers maniacally wield overloaded carts, indifferent to shy customers. But the bold and the badgered agree that this is the city's most authentic dim sum.

☎ 296-7733 ✉ 644 Broadway ⌚ 10:30am-3pm & 5-9:30pm Mon-Fri, 8am-3pm & 5-9:30pm Sat & Sun 🚌 15, 30, 41, 45 ♿ ♿

House of Nanking (5, C4) $
Chinese

You'll feel instantly greasy as soon as you step into this nondescript closet, a favorite of cubicle dwellers. Despite the dine-and-dash ambience, Nanking does great pot stickers and mu shu pork. If you're on a leisurely schedule, avoid the crowds and hit the Nanking between 2pm and 5pm. Cash only.

☎ 421-1429 ✉ 919 Kearny St ⌚ 11am-10pm

Head to Chinatown's Gold Mountain for authenic dim sum

Mon-Sat, noon-9pm Sun Ⓜ Montgomery St 🚌 1, 15, 41 Ⓥ ♿

Hunan Home's (5, C4) $
Chinese

Dolled up like a pink-and-white prom queen, Hunan Home's is consistently crowned the best Chinese in San Francisco. Stir-fried string beans and garlic chicken are just a few of the spicy Hunan-style dishes that please the court. The busy wonton soup is accompanied by a preparation of a tasty chili, soy and plum sauce.

☎ 982-2844 ✉ 622 Jackson St ⌚ 11:30am-9:30pm Sun-Thu, to 10pm Fri & Sat 🚌 1, 15, 41 Ⓟ validated

parking at Portsmouth Square Garage after 5pm ♿ Ⓥ ♿

Yuet Lee (5, B3) $
Chinese

With lime green walls and abusive fluorescent lighting, Yuet Lee skips decor in favor of flavor. Among its Hong Kong—style seafood dishes, flounder in black bean sauce and salt-and-pepper crab attract Bay Area chefs and regular nobodies. For the late night crowd, suitably salty dishes of crispy chow mein scratch the post-drinking itch. Cash only.

☎ 982-6020 ✉ 1300 Stockton St ⌚ 11am-3am Wed-Sun 🚌 15, 30, 41, 45 ♿ Ⓥ ♿

Dim Sum Fun

C'mon, let's be honest – who really understands the rules of the dim sum game? How do you know what's in those bamboo baskets? Once you gamble on a few, do you still wonder if the 'sum' in dim sum stands for 'steamed unidentified morsels'?

First, dim sum is a morning thing, and the earlier you arrive, the better it is. There are two types of restaurants – hole-in-the-walls for take-away or quick gobbling, and fancy banquet affairs courting either Chinese or Western tastes. If you're new to dim sum and don't want a commitment, head to **Good Luck Dim Sum** (p76). If gourmet is your style, head to **Yank Sing** (p78), **Harbor Village** (p67) or **Ton Kiang Restaurant** (p76). If you've dim summed before, then you are ready for the cultural immersion at **Gold Mountain** (above).

CIVIC CENTER & HAYES VALLEY

Absinthe (6, C5) $$$
French
More Parisian than the French, Absinthe sets a belle epoque table with a dining room of octagonal-tiled floor, copper-top bar and picture windows. Dissenters criticize the moody service and textbook French cuisine, but opinions converge on a brunch of Niman ranch burgers and banana-blueberry pancakes.
☎ 551-1590 ✉ 398 Hayes St ⏱ 11:30am-3pm & 5pm-midnight Tue-Thu, 11:30am midnight Fri, 10:30am-midnight Sat, 10:30am-10:30pm Sun; bar open to 2am, except Sun 🚌 21 Ⓥ ♿

Citizen Cake (6, C5) $$
California
Baker Elizabeth Falkner is a former art student whose cakes and cookies bear the stamp of a woman weaned on abstract expressionists. The light meals from chef Jennifer Cox are solid interpretations of French classics, with offerings such as a winter salad of baby spinach, pancetta and poached egg.
☎ 861-2228 ✉ 399 Grove St ⏱ 8am-10pm

Tue-Fri, 10am-10pm Sat, 10am-5pm Sun (to 9pm on performance nights)
🚊 K, L, M, N lines to Van Ness, F line, 5, 21, 47, 49 Ⓥ ♿

Fritz (6, C5) $
European
In this European-style coffee house, Belgian fries are served in a parfait glass with a choice of dipping sauces (pesto mayonnaise or strawberry mustard) – an exotic innovation to the monotonous ketchup bath. An odd partner to the fries, the salads are terrific, and a huge selection of wines

and beers can be enjoyed on the mossy backyard patio.
☎ 864-7654 ✉ 579 Hayes St ⏱ 9am-10pm Sun-Thu, to midnight Fri & Sat 🚌 21 ♿ Ⓥ ♿

Hayes St Grill (6, C5) $$$
Seafood
The menu at this pre-theater staging room is straightforward with barely molested fish served in an equally spartan dining room. No fuss and no need to ask about unpronounceables on the menu. For sympathetic eaters, most fish are sustainably harvested, like the Ventura

Devour Absinthe's authentic French cuisine

The Must (Not the Musty) List
This list is a cross section of the types of cuisines where San Francisco excels:
Zuni Café (p66) For California cuisine.
Slanted Door (p78) For contemporary Vietnamese.
Ebisu (p76) For sushi.
Taquería Pancho Villa (p72) For burritos.
Yank Sing (p78) For dim sum.
Ferry Building Marketplace (p77) For weekend and local harvest grazing.

County harpoon-caught swordfish – it's a mouthful.
☎ 863-5545 ✉ 320 Hayes St ⏲ 11:30am-2pm & 5-9:30pm Mon-Thu, 11:30am-2pm & 5-10:30pm Fri, 5:30-10:30pm Sat, 5-8:30pm Sun 🚇 K, L, M, N lines to Van Ness, F line, 21, 47, 49 Ⓥ ♿

Il Borgo (6, C5) $$
Italian
Around the corner from Hayes Valley's pretentious gourmet gulch, this neighborhood restaurant is full of Italian comforts, including kitschy candles melted into Dali-esque sculptures. Hearty homemade pastas are delivered with maternal concern by the waitstaff.
☎ 255-9108 ✉ 500 Fell St ⏲ 5:30-10pm 🚇 21 ♿ Ⓥ ♿

Zuni Café (6, C5) $$$
California
Like Rick's in Casablanca, everyone comes to Zuni, with its long copper bar and pie-shaped dining room ensconced in windows. Small dishes of intense flavors demonstrate the bounty of California's long growing season. Oysters and roast chicken for two fresh from Zuni's brick oven are its signature dishes.
☎ 552-2522 ✉ 1658 Market St ⏲ 11:30am-midnight Tue-Sat, 11am-11pm Sun 🚇 F line, 6, 7, 66, 71 ♿ Ⓥ ♿

DOWNTOWN

Aqua (5, D4) $$$$
Seafood
With its emphasis squarely on seafood, Aqua dominates San Francisco's fascination with French-California offsprings. For an added adventure, the dishes are sometimes infused with wanderlust, like the Moroccan spiced ahi tuna tartare. Heralded as a power lunch restaurant, the austere dining room echoes noise like a train tunnel.
☎ 956-9662 ✉ 252 California St ⏲ 11:30am-2pm & 5.30-10:30pm Mon-Thu, 11:30am-2pm & 5-11pm Fri, 5-11pm Sat 🚇 Embarcadero 🚋 California St cable car, 1, 2, 3, 4 Ⓥ ♿

B-44 (5, C5) $$
Catalan
Tapas are usually terribly overrated in San Francisco. But here in the European outpost of Belden Place, this Catalan bistro expertly executes *jamon serrano* (dry-cured ham), roast rabbit, and a chicken and monkfish combo. Avoid it on crowded weekend nights, and embrace it when the outdoor tables form a boisterous party.
☎ 986-6287 ✉ 44 Belden Pl ⏲ 11:30am-2:30pm Mon-Fri, 5:30pm-midnight Mon-Sat 🚇 Montgomery St 🚌 15, 30, 45 ♿ Ⓥ ♿

Banh Mi Saigon (5, A6) $
Vietnamese
Mini submarine-shaped Vietnamese sandwiches with pâté, grated cucumbers, carrots and peppers are sold alongside daily sundries at this humble storefront in the newly christened 'Little Saigon' area of the Tenderloin. Many of the Vietnamese immigrants were resettled

here after the Vietnam War. Here's to half-baked foreign policy and crusty baguettes.
☎ 474-5698 ✉ 560 Larkin St ☯ 6:30am-5pm Mon-Sat, 7:30am-4:30pm Sun 🚌 19, 31 ♿

Blondie's (5, C6) $
American
In the great American pizza showdown, San Francisco isn't even invited. Nonetheless, Blondie's thick, gooey slices are Downtown's best gulp-and-go bargain. As you stand on the sidewalk devouring a huge slice to stave off cold and delirium, you'll realize somewhere after the fifth bite that this is good pizza.
☎ 982-6168 ✉ 51 Powell St ☯ 11am-6pm Ⓜ Powell St 🚌 F line ♿ Ⓥ ♿

Campton Place (5, C5) $$$$
French-California
Wrapped up like a holiday chocolate, Campton Place is hailed as one of the best hotel restaurants in the country. Southwestern France debuts alongside California cuisine and the city's best selection of artisanal cheeses. There are special food and wine pairings for serious gastronomes. Jackets required.
☎ 955-5555 ✉ 340 Stockton St ☯ breakfast, lunch & dinner; call for reservations Ⓜ Powell St 🚌 2, 3, 4, 30 Ⓥ ♿

Fleur de Lys (5, B5) $$$$
French
Fairytale-style romance, Fleur de Lys is a high cuisine circus performed in a silken

San Francisco's café culture hard at work

big top. Traditional French – buttery sauces, silky lobster, herbaceous lamb and divine pastries – take hours to transpire, like a vivid dream.
☎ 673-7779 ✉ 777 Sutter St ☯ 6:30-9:30pm Mon-Thu, 5:30-10:30pm Fri & Sat 🚌 2, 3, 4 Ⓥ ♿

Harbor Village (5, D4) $$
Chinese
With views of the bay and the Embarcadero, Harbor Village serves up an impressive dim sum lunch and Cantonese seafood dinner. This is the US outpost of waterfront restaurants anchored back in Kowloon. The always popular shrimp and pea shoot dumplings make extra rounds during the dim sum parade.
☎ 781-8833 ✉ 4 Embarcadero Center ☯ 11am-2:30pm & 5:30-9:30pm Mon-Fri, 10:30am-2:30pm & 5:30-9:30pm Sat & Sun Ⓜ Embarcadero 🚌 California St cable car, 1, 41 ♿ Ⓥ ♿

Jeanty at Jack's (5, C4) $$$
French
Acclaimed Yountville chef Philippe Jeanty has resurrected the historic Jack's bistro, once a martini powerbroker club. The menu is traditional French fare, with a divine tomato soup capped with puff pastry, exquisite steak frites and cassoulet. Regulars advise that dinner is more charming than lunch.
☎ 693-0941 ✉ 615 Sacramento St ☯ 11:30am-10:30pm Mon-Thu, 11:30am-11:30pm Fri, 5-11:30pm Sat & Sun Ⓜ Montgomery St 🚌 1, 15, 41 ♿

Masa's (5, C5) $$$$
French
Bored by celebrity chefs? What if he was the only American to win an 'Iron Chef' challenge? Meet your new idol, Masa's Ron Siegel, who beat the in-house French Iron Chef in 1998 (sorry, Bobby Flay). Widely regarded as one of the city's

best, Masa's has a revolving menu honoring truffles, duck breast and other French delicacies. Jackets required.

☎ 989-7154 ✉ 648 Bush St ⏰ 5:30-9:30pm Tue-Sat 🚋 Powell-Mason & Powell-Hyde cable cars Ⓥ ♿

Mocca on Maiden Lane (5, C5) $
American
Just off Union Square, Mocca has outdoor tables serenaded by a jazz trio. It offers light fare, such as pasta salads, fishbowl-sized café au laits and London broil sandwiches served on a baguette with enough gravy to redefine the term 'French dip.'

☎ 956-1188 ✉ 175 Maiden Ln ⏰ 10:30am-5:30pm Ⓜ Powell St

🚌 2, 3, 4, 30, 45 🚶 Ⓥ ♿

Piperade (5, C3) $$
Basque
With exposed rafters and knobby furnishings, Piperade transforms an industrial warehouse into a rustic barn from a simpler time. The mood is informal, the staff psychic, and the food glorious. The white bean salad with anchovies invokes the Basque tradition of communal cooking. Dinner is less crowded than lunch.

☎ 391-2555 ✉ 1015 Battery St ⏰ 11:30am-2:30pm & 5:30-10:30pm Mon-Sat 🚌 10 Ⓥ ♿

Plouf (5, C5) $$
French Seafood
It smells like the ocean in this tiled restaurant known for its mussels served eight

different ways and other French-inflected seafood stews and grills. Part of the Belden Place parade of restaurants, Plouf (French for 'splash') is worth diving into on a warm sunny day when the outdoor tables form a communal picnic.

☎ 986-6491 ✉ 40 Belden Pl ⏰ 11am-3pm & 5:30-10pm Mon-Fri, 5:30-11pm Sat Ⓜ Montgomery St 🚌 2, 3, 4 ♿

Rubicon (5, C4) $$$$
French-California
From the people who brought Nobu and Montrachet to New York comes this fine French restaurant with a unique Californian edge. The veal chops wrapped in grape leaves, John Dory wrapped in paper and a wine list with 40 wines under $40 are meant to impress.

What Is California Cuisine?
The term 'California cuisine' is so widely defined that it often refers to almost any fusion food. One constant, however, is modest portions (a euphemism for 'small'). If you leave the table still a little hungry, then congratulations, you've just had California cuisine.

The paneled rooms have the understated confidence of a men's club.
☎ 434-4100 ✉ 558 Sacramento St
🕑 11:30am-2:30pm Wed, 5:30-10:30pm Mon-Sat 🅜 Montgomery St
🚌 1, 15, 45 🅥 ♿

Sam's Grill (5, C5) $$$
Seafood
Many a hungry, swaggering Bonanza King have filled the wooden booths at Sam's Grill. In homage to striking it rich, Sam's serves the Gold Rush mascot, the hangtown fry, a power-fully rich omelete made of bacon, oysters, eggs and heavy cream – created by a successful gold panner who requested a concoction of all the fanciest ingredients he could possibly think of.
☎ 421-0594 ✉ 374 Bush St 🕑 11am-9pm Mon-Fri 🅜 Montgomery St
🚌 15, 30, 45 🚶 🅥 ♿

Sears Fine Food (5, B5) $
American
This coffee shop has served '12 little pancakes' to visitors since the 1930s. Its draw is partly its location in the area surrounding Union Square, and partly the charm of walking into a modest time warp for an adequate, inexpensive breakfast or lunch.
☎ 986-1190 ✉ 439 Powell St 🕑 6:30am-2:30pm 🅜 Powell St
🚌 Powell-Mason & Powell-Hyde cable cars, 2, 3, 4 ♿ ♿

Shalimar (5, B6) $
Indian-Pakistani
Indifferent to its unsavory location and to its customers, Shalimar operates by a strict credo – 'No alterations for local tastes and no frills.' Met by flamboyant spices and a sulking pit crew of fry cooks, you order at the counter, help yourself to water and

sauces in the cold case and listen for your number to be called. BYOB and cash only.
☎ 928-0333
✉ 532 Jones St
🕑 noon-3pm, 5:30-11:30pm 🚌 2, 3, 4, 38
🚶 🅥 ♿

Tadich Grill (5, D4) $$
Seafood
Established in 1849, this is San Francisco's oldest restaurant. Step back in time to the black-and-white days of yore centered around a U-shaped counter for solo and unfussy dining, and taciturn waiters wearing an air of laboratory precision. The menu is a subdued old-timer with daily fresh fish. Avoid downtown lunch times.
☎ 391-1849
✉ 240 California St
🕑 11am-9:30pm Mon-Fri, 11:30am-9:30pm Sat 🅜 Embarcadero
🚌 California St cable car, 1 🅥 ♿

THE HAIGHT

Cha Cha Cha (2, E2) $$
Caribbean
A jungle of potted plants and sweet tropical drinks create a festive mood at this popular neighborhood tapas bar, a favorite with groups of friends. Inside the little dishes drawn from Mexico and the Islands create the impres-sion of a tropical oasis while outside the evening blanket of fog descends on the valley.
☎ 386-7670 ✉ 1801 Haight St 🕑 11:30am-4pm & 5-11pm 🚌 N line, 6, 7, 43, 71 ♿

Citrus Club (2, F2) $
Asian
This informal noodle house rescues Haight St from restaurant mediocrity. Huge steamy bowls of noodles with wedges of tofu and parboiled vegetables take the chill off a foggy day and require Zen-like patience to consume. Other dishes from Thailand and Vietnam get menu roles with fresh and colorful arrangements.
☎ 387-6366 ✉ 1790 Haight St 🕑 11:30am-10pm Sun-Thu, to 11pm Fri & Sat 🚌 N line, 6, 7, 43, 71 🚶 🅥 ♿

EOS Restaurant & Wine Bar (2, F3) $$$
Fusion
Some of the best fusion cooking in all of San Francisco can be found on this back street on the edge of the Haight. Try the inspired tangerine peel braised osso bucco, or perhaps the tea smoked duck breast with mashed potatoes. Or simply come for an adventure at the wine bar.
☎ 566-3063 ✉ 901 Carl St 🕑 5:30-10pm Sun-Thu, to 11pm Fri & Sat 🚌 N line, 43 🅥 ♿

After Hours

Need more than a slice of pizza in the wee hours? **Absinthe** (p65) serves a modified bar menu until late. A favorite with the restaurant set, **Yuet Lee** (p64) in Chinatown stays open till a scandalous 3am. Just like in the movies, San Francisco teens while away a late night at **Mel's Drive In** (p75), and the aging teen spirit can be found at **Balboa Café** (p75).

Indian Oven (6, B5) $

Indian

Playing to all the subcontinental fantasies of a Raj's palace, Indian Oven reigns as a date place for novice couples. Tandoori dishes or the mixed tandoori special may not be conducive to smooching, but the devoted fans waiting patiently in line don't seem to care. Service is notoriously slow.
☎ 626-1628 ✉ 233 Fillmore St ⏱ 5-11pm 🚆 J, N lines, 6, 7, 22, 66, 71 ♿ Ⓥ ♿

Kate's Kitchen (6, B5) $

American

A neighborhood breakfast favorite, Kate's Kitchen serves up platter-size pancakes piled high with fruits, as well as a range of other breakfast standards to fuel all those over-achieving weekend warriors.
☎ 626-3984 ✉ 471 Haight St ⏱ 8am-9pm Mon-Fri, 9am-9pm Sat, 9am-4pm Sun 🚆 J, N lines, 6, 7, 22, 66, 71 ♿ ♿

Rosamunde Grill (6, B5) $

Sausages

In a city that has designer pizzas it's no surprise to find a designer sausage stand, with German wursts from knocks to bocks. Grilled to perfection in front of you, there are a few stools in the cramped space, or go next door to Toronado (p83) for a beef and beer fest.
☎ 437-6851 ✉ 545 Haight St ⏱ 11:30am-10pm 🚆 J, N lines , 6, 7, 22, 66, 71 ♿ ♿

Indian Oven's subcontinental delights are worth the wait on busy nights

THE MISSION

Blowfish Sushi (3, E4) $$
Japanese

With the cocky slogan 'sushi to die for,' Blowfish is often misunderstood. Handrolls and sashimi, the obvious definition of 'sushi,' play only a minor role here. Artistic fusion dishes (like pyramid of tartare, a 3D construction of avocado and raw tuna) and potent sake cocktails are the superheroes in this video game environment of pulsating techno music and frenetic anime cartoons.

☎ 285-3848
✉ 2170 Bryant St
🕐 11:30am-2:30pm & 5:30-10:30pm Mon-Fri, 5:30-10:30pm Sat & Sun
🚌 9, 27 Ⓥ ♿

Burger Joint (4, C2) $
American

Even when it comes to the guilty pleasures of red meat, San Franciscans ardently demand healthy and enviro-friendly options. Local Niman Ranch beef burgers, free-range chickens and all-beef hot dogs take some of the fun out of junk food, but it does add a lot more flavor. Cash only.

☎ 824-3494 ✉ 807 Valencia St 🕐 11am-11pm
🚌 26, 33, 49 Ⓥ ♿

Foreign Cinema (4, C3) $$
French

Through the fortress-like metal doors is a boisterous scene of picnic tables arranged around an outdoor courtyard where foreign films are screened. Often sold as a cross between fine dining and a drive-in, the artful French fare is indeed

Dine inside or out at the Foreign Cinema

fine, but the movies are wallpaper for overstimulated techno geeks.

☎ 648-7600 ✉ 2534 Mission St 🕐 5:30pm-2am Tue-Sun Ⓜ 24th St
🚌 14, 26, 49 Ⓥ ♿

Herbivore (4, C3) $
Vegetarian-Vegan

With all the haute vegetarian restaurants in town, one might fear that meatless has forsaken the huddled masses. Never fear, Herbivore is here. A relaxed café with working-stiff prices, Herbivore has a varied menu of veggie and dairy-free adaptations of international extractions. There is another branch in the Western Addition (6, A5; 531 Divisadero St).

☎ 826-5657 ✉ 983 Valencia St 🕐 11am-10pm Sun-Thu, to 11pm Fri & Sat
🚌 14, 26, 49 ♿ Ⓥ ♿

La Corneta (4, C3) $
Mexican

Breaking with the traditional taquería mold,

squeaky-clean La Corneta looks like a refugee from an upscale Mexico City shopping mall. Commanded by an attractive staff, La Corneta does the best grilled prawn and fish tacos this side of Baja.

☎ 643-7001 ✉ 2731 Mission St 🕐 11am-10pm
Ⓜ 24th St 🚌 14, 49
♿ Ⓥ ♿

La Taquería (4, C4) $
Mexican

For *carne asada* (grilled flank steak), tacos that are light and fresh, La Taquería steams its tortillas, makes the best guacamole in town and grills its meats without the mid-bite oil spill. Don't make the mistake of most 'tourists' (from other neighborhoods) by ordering the lackluster burritos, but do opt for an *aquas frescas* (fruit drink).

☎ 285-7117 ✉ 2889 Mission St 🕐 11am-9pm Mon-Sat, to 8pm Sun
Ⓜ 24th St 🚌 14, 48, 49
♿ Ⓥ ♿

Pauline's Pizza (4, B1) $
Pizzeria

This is the home of designer pizza in San Francisco, with crusts as thin as a fashion model and dressed up with toppings such as chicken sausage, Louisiana andouille or thin-sliced potatoes with green olives.

☎ 552-2050 ✉ 260 Valencia St ◷ 5-10pm Tue-Sat Ⓜ 16th St ⊒ 14, 26, 49 ⟨⟩ Ⓥ ⟨⟩

St Francis Fountain (3, E4) $
American

A Mission District treasure, St Francis Fountain has been in operation since 1918 and has maintained its impeccable soda fountain appearance. Inexpensive burgers and sandwiches are on the menu, but St Francis' forte is its ice-cream and malted milk shakes.

☎ 826-4200 ✉ 2801 24th St ◷ 11am-9pm Mon-Fri, 11:30am-8pm Sat & Sun ⊒ 9, 27, 48 ⟨⟩ ⟨⟩

Taquería Pancho Villa (4, C2) $
Mexican

Burrito virgins, please step this way. Join the line that snakes alongside a grill of sizzling meat and a chopping block where *carne asada* is hacked into bite-size bits. Near the mariachi band is a self-serve salsa bar boasting half a dozen concoctions that win Pancho Villa blue ribbons at the state fair.

☎ 864-8840 ✉ 3071 16th St ◷ 10am-midnight Ⓜ 16th St ⊒ 14, 22, 26, 49 ⟨⟩ Ⓥ ⟨⟩

Go Mexican in the Mission

Tartine (4, B2) $
Bakery

This chic bakery-café proves that you don't have to be a crunchy hippie to be organic. Amid wi-fi surfers and urban hipsters, Tartine's good-earth politics (natural ingredients from local farms) merge effortlessly with artisanal sensibilities. Fresh-baked pastries and a custardy bread pudding are so 'healthy' you'll fly through your morning.

☎ 487-2600 ✉ 600 Guerrero St ◷ 7:30am-7pm Tue-Fri, 8am-7pm Sat, 9am-7pm Sun ⊒ J line, 26, 33 ⟨⟩ Ⓥ ⟨⟩

Ti Couz (4, B2) $$
Crêperie

With its sunny patio and white-washed interior, Ti Couz resembles its humble French translation 'the old house.' The menu includes over 60 kinds of sweet and savory crepes, all made according to the Brittany tradition. This place is well-known among locals, so be prepared to wait for a table.

☎ 252-7373 ✉ 3108 16th St ◷ 11am-11pm Mon-Fri, 10am-11pm Sat, 10am-10pm Sun Ⓜ 16th St ⊒ 14, 22, 26, 49 ⟨⟩ Ⓥ ⟨⟩

Burrito Business

Have you been formally introduced to the Mission burrito? While burritos exist elsewhere, this Latino neighborhood has perfected the self-contained meal. As big as a man's forearm, burritos can be stuffed with hundreds of combinations (hot or mild salsa, black or refried beans, grilled, stewed or deep-fried meat or veggies), and there are hundreds of taquerías with different specialities. Like shoes were to Imelda, taquerías are to Mission-grazers, and comparing notes elicits great debate, respect or disgust (much like New Yorkers and pizza).

A point of mass agreement is the technique for consuming a burrito: take the foil wrapped package and turn it on one end, peeling the foil down with each bite. This way the fillings don't escape and you can wrap it up when you relent and cry 'tio.'

NORTH BEACH & RUSSIAN HILL

Helmand (5, C3) $$

Afghan

Afghan cuisine is a meeting place for the flavors of India and Persia, and the city's best ambassador, Helmand, is like a well-dressed matron amid the bawdy strip clubs on Broadway. Try the lamb dishes or the sweet pumpkin with yogurt sauce with a finale of strong Turkish coffee.

☎ 362-0641 ✉ 430 Broadway ⏱ 5:30-10pm Tue-Thu, to 11pm Fri & Sat 🚌 12, 15, 30, 41 ♿ Ⓥ ♿

Mario's Bohemian Cigar Store Café (5, B3) $

Italian

Shake off a foggy day or plot your afternoon's course at this park-side café. Once a neighborhood card club, Mario's serves hot focaccia sandwiches and to-die-for biscotti. For late-risers Mario's sandwiches might be their only chance to try focaccia from the famous **Liguria Bakery** (5, B3; 1700 Stockton St; ⏱ 8am-2pm Mon-Sun).

☎ 362-0536 ✉ 566 Columbus Ave ⏱ 10am-11pm 🚌 15, 30, 39, 41, 45 ♿ Ⓥ ♿

Molinari Delicatessen (5, C3) $

Italian

The neighborhood's great deli weaned many of the hearty residents on a diet of meats, cheeses and pastas. Crusty sandwiches are made for take-away orders.

☎ 421-2337 ✉ 373 Columbus Ave ⏱ 8am-6pm Mon-Fri, 7:30am-5:30pm Sat 🚌 15, 30, 45 ♿ ♿

Rose Pistola (5, B3) $$$

Italian

This is not your grandma's trattoria, but it could easily pass for a cosmopolitan cousin's breezy bistro. Representing the northern region of Liguria (part of the Italian Riviera), Rose Pistola is one of North Beach's best Italian restaurants with a 'but.' The kitchen excels at grilled seafood (such as the superb Monterey squid) but fumbles with pasta.

☎ 399-0499 ✉ 532 Columbus Ave ⏱ 11:30am-11pm Sun-Thu, 11am-midnight Fri & Sat 🚌 15, 30, 41, 45 ♿ Ⓥ ♿

Sodini's Trattoria (5, C3) $

Italian

This family-owned restaurant is a neighborhood favorite offering dependable and generous Northern Italian fare (from raviolis to veal scaloppine). Everyone seems to know each other, especially at the bar, which mixes up its own house cocktails (try the Liz Taylor).

☎ 291-0499 ✉ 510 Green St ⏱ 5-10pm 🚌 15, 41 ♿

Stella Pastry and Café (5, C3) $

Italian pastries

Stellas is known for its St Honore cake and other Italian pastries and cookies. Another indulgence is their

Join the locals at Mario's Bohemian Cigar Store Café

A Mouthful of a View

The walk up Russian Hill isn't enough of a view – you want more? For dining views, try the **Waterfront Restaurant & Café** (p78), **Harbor Village** (p67), **Beach Chalet** (p32) and **Red's Java House** (p77).

scripantina, a rich sponge cake with liqueur and cream.

☎ 986-2914
✉ 446 Columbus Ave
🕑 7:30am-6pm Oct-May, to 10pm Jun-Sep
🚌 15, 30, 41, 45 🚶 ♿

Café Roma (5, B3) $

Café

The unofficial saint in this neighborhood is St Sidewalk as evidenced by all the sidewalk cafés and their devotees. With outdoor tables on quiet Stockton St, Café Roma is the preferred spot of locals with lots of staff shout-outs to regulars.

☎ 296-7942
✉ 526 Columbus Ave
🕑 6am-7pm Mon-Thu,

6am-8pm Fri, 7am-midnight Sat, 7am-8pm Sun 🚌 15, 30, 41, 45
🚶 ♿

La Folie (6, C2) $$$$

French

Jacques Pepin sometimes comes here for dinner when he's filming one of his cooking shows at KQED-TV. Roland Passot's fine French hand is in evidence whether you order à la carte (try the snails or veal chop) or the five-course discovery meal.

☎ 776-5577
✉ 2316 Polk St
🕑 5:30-10pm Mon-Sat
🚌 Powell-Hyde cable car, 19, 41, 45, 47, 49 ♿

Swan Oyster Depot (6, C3) $

Seafood

Once a fish market, this restaurant is now operated by the gregarious Sancimino brothers as an old-school raw bar. A line often stretches down the block for the coveted stools along the marble counter. Fresh, sea-salty oysters on the half shell, cracked Dungeness crab and the signature crab Louie will keep you busy. This place is cash only.

☎ 673-1101 ✉ 1517 Polk St 🕑 8am-5:30pm Mon-Sat 🚌 California St cable car, 1, 19, 47, 49
Ⓥ ♿ no

Step into your own version of *American Graffiti* with a burger and malt at Mel's Drive-In

PACIFIC HEIGHTS, MARINA DISTRICT & JAPANTOWN

Balboa Café (6, B2) $$
American
This old boy's club of brass railings and moulded ceilings is in the midst of a late-life crisis as the young breeders of Pac Heights come here to spawn. (This corner is called the Bermuda Triangle because so many singles 'disappear' into the night.) A late night menu with hearty burgers are solace if you're still solo.
☎ 921-3944 ✉ 3199 Fillmore St ⏱ 11:30am-10pm Mon-Wed, 11am-2am Thu-Sat, 10am-10pm Sun 🚌 22, 41, 45 ♿

Betelnut (6, B2) $$
Pan-Asian
Betelnut seductively combines pan-Asian cuisine with an exotic 1930s film noir atmosphere. Start off with a home brewed beer and some 'little plates' – such as green papaya salad and chili crusted calamari. Don't miss the sea bass with black sesame seeds.
☎ 929-8855 ✉ 2030 Union St ⏱ 11:30am-11pm Sun-Thu, to midnight Fri & Sat 🚌 22, 41, 45 🚴 Ⓥ ♿

Extreme Pizza (6, B4) $
Pizzeria
With gourmet leanings, these creatively themed pizzas (Holy Cow!, Mr Pestato Head) are overloaded with gorgonzola, fresh basil, baby spinach and even hummus (Peace in the Middle East). Also located in **Pacific Heights** (6, B2; ☎ 929-8234; 1980 Union St) and **South of**

Market (5, C7; ☎ 701-9000; 1052 Folsom St).
☎ 929-9900 ✉ 1730 Fillmore St ⏱ 9am-6pm Mon-Fri, 11am-3pm Sat 🚌 2, 3, 4, 22 🚴 Ⓥ ♿

Greens (6, B1) $$$
Vegetarian
At this long-standing vegetarian restaurant, gourmet goes meatless with a seasonal menu harvested from Green Gulch farm in Marin County. Veggie lasagna, spicy curries and a stellar brunch appeal to the Betty Crocker School as well as the New Age ashram. Surely the generous view of the Golden Gate Bridge has something to do with it?
☎ 771-6222 ✉ Fort Mason Center, Bldg A, Marina Blvd ⏱ 11:30am-2:30pm & 5:30-9:30pm Tue-Sat, 10:30am-2pm Sun, 5:30-9:30pm 🚌 22 Ⓟ 🚴 Ⓥ ♿

Mel's Drive-In (6, B2) $
American
Playing a supporting role in George Lucas' *American Graffiti*, Mel's embodies 1950s car culture with standbys like burgers, malts and fries. Other branches: **South of Market** (5, C6; ☎ 227-4477; 801 Mission St) and **Civic Center** (5, A5; ☎ 292-6357; 1050 Van Ness Ave).
☎ 921-3039 ✉ 2165 Lombard St ⏱ 24hr 🚌 22, 30, 76 Ⓟ 🚴 Ⓥ ♿

Vegetarian Paradise
When the rest of the country is in a deep freeze, California harvests asparagus and artichokes, then strawberries and cherries, and later tomatoes and basil. **Greens** (above) and **Herbivore** (p71) specialize in preparing these and other local beauties, but interesting veggie dishes can be found at most restaurants. Salads are also serious business here, so if you happen to encounter a bad one, complain directly to the mayor.

Mifune (6, B4) $
Japanese

Inside forlorn Japan Center, this traditional-style noodle house does a wallet-friendly lunch special. Try the *udon* (wheat noodles) or the *soba* (buckwheat noodles) with your choice of toppings from seaweed to fish cakes. Another branch, **Mifune Don** (6, B4; ☎ 346-1993, 22 Peace Plaza) is reportedly better but has less atmosphere.
☎ 922-0337

Mifune's pictorial menu

✉ Kintetsu Mall, Japan Center, 1737 Post St
🕙 11am-11pm
🚌 2, 3, 4, 38 👤 Ⓥ ♿

On the Bridge (6, B4) $
Japanese

A squat shop on the bridge between Japan Center's Kintetsu and Kinokuniya buildings proves that foreigners did sneak into the isolated kingdom. Known as *yo-sho-ku-ya*, curry from India and pasta from Europe were integrated into the cuisine more than 100 years ago.
☎ 922-7765 ✉ Japan Center, 1581 Webster St
🕙 11:30am-10pm
🚌 2, 3, 4, 38 👤 Ⓥ ♿

THE RICHMOND & THE SUNSET

Arizmendi Bakery (2, D3) $
Pizzeria

Named after a Basque priest who organized worker collectives, Arizmendi makes a dreamy sourdough-crust pizza, pastries and peasant loaves of bread. Worker-owned, the little take-away shop gives discounts if you ride your bike or take the bus here.
☎ 566-3117 ✉ 1331 9th Ave 🕙 7am-7pm Tue-Fri, 8am-7pm Sat, 8am-4pm Sun 🚌 N line, 6, 29, 43 👤 Ⓥ ♿

Ebisu (2, D3) $
Japanese

Taking no chances with its traditional sushi house decor, Ebisu reserves its rebellion for its creative hand roll menu. The swamp roll (tuna and seaweed salad) and the Louisiana hot roll (bonita and hot sauce) as well as top-notch sashimi and *nigiri* coax from the wasabi-addicted hordes the competitive title of best sushi in town.
☎ 566-1770 ✉ 1283 9th Ave 🕙 5-10pm Mon-Wed, 5-11pm Thu & Fri, 11:30am-10pm Sat & Sun 🚌 N line, 6, 29, 43 👤 Ⓥ ♿

Good Luck Dim Sum (2, D1) $
Chinese

Part of the satellite Chinatown along Clement St, Good Luck finally explains the differences between all those identical pieces of dim sum dough with its handy menu. Standouts include garlicky chive dumplings and mysteriously named crystal dumplings. Mark your order clearly on the paper slip and expect a little abuse from the counter.
☎ 386-3388 ✉ 736 Clement St 🕙 7am-6:30pm Wed-Mon
🚌 2, 38 👤 ♿

Ton Kiang Restaurant (2, C1) $$
Chinese

Easier on the wallet than Embarcadero's Yank Sing (p78), this Sunset restaurant does dim sum for the masses. The Chinese greens are fantastic and their other Cantonese dishes include a succulent black cod with black bean sauce.
☎ 387-8275
✉ 5821 Geary Blvd
🕙 10:30am-10pm Mon-Thu, 10:30am-10:30pm Fri, 10am-10:30pm Sat, 9am-10:30pm Sun
🚌 38 👤 Ⓥ ♿

Big Dinner Deals
If you're looking for the Goldilocks business dinner (not too simple, not too expensive, not too quiet, not too dull), try **Aqua** (p66), **Boulevard** (opposite), **Rubicon** (p68) or **Campton Place** (p67).

SOUTH OF MARKET & EMBARCADERO

Acme Chophouse (5, E7) $$$
American

A steakhouse with an environmental agenda, yeah right. Traci Des Jardins of Jardiniere has successfully mated these incongruous species by serving locally raised grass-fed beef, oysters and delicious sides that even a Republican could love. Only the spotty service will disappoint.

☎ 644-0240 ✉ SBC Park, 24 Willie Mays Plaza ⏰ 5-10:30pm Sun-Wed, to 11pm Thu-Sat, 10:30am-10:30pm game days 🚌 F line, 10, 15, 30, 45 ♿

Basil (5, B8) $$
Thai

The smell of fish sauce, not faux traditional decor, is an immediate indicator of a proficient Thai restaurant. As cosmopolitan as a Bangkok bilingual, Basil creatively adapts Thai cuisine to California ingredients without insulting either – a diplomatic deed. Don't miss the spicy beef salad and intense green curry.

☎ 552-8999 ✉ 1175 Folsom St ⏰ 11:30am-2:45pm & 5-10pm Mon-Fri, 5-10:30pm Sat & Sun 🚌 12, 19 ♿ Ⓥ ♿

Boulevard (5, E4) $$$$
Contemporary American

Boulevard's belle epoque ambience and elegant dishes cause San Franciscans to gush with praise and lovestruck enthusiasm. Chef Nancy Oakes delivers a seasonal menu of savory pork loins or pan roasted duck breast on corn cakes and mounds of buttery mashed potatoes. Reservations essential.

☎ 543-6084 ✉ 1 Mission St, Audiffred Bldg ⏰ 11:30am-2pm & 5:30-10pm Mon-Fri, 5:30-10pm Sat & Sun Ⓜ Embarcadero 🚌 F line, 2, 7, 9, 14, 66, 71 Ⓥ ♿

Ferry Building Marketplace (5, E4) $$
California

The old ferry building has been transformed into a showplace for artisanal food products from northern California. Come to sample the goat cheeses from Cowgirl Creamery, Italian sandwiches from Mastrelli's Delicatessen, oysters from Hog Island Oyster Company, and wine at Ferry Plaza Wine Merchants. Along with half the city, you can also forage for a light weekend brunch at the affiliated farmer's market (p52); just buy coffee before arriving as there is usually a shortage.

✉ Market & Embarcadero ⏰ 10am-6pm Mon-Fri, 9am-6pm Sat, 11am-5pm Sun Ⓜ Embarcadero 🚌 F line ⛴ Blue & Gold and Golden Gate from Tiburon, Sausalito, Oakland & Alameda Ⓟ Pier 1/2 & Washington-Embarcadero lots ♿ Ⓥ ♿

Hawthorne Lane (5, D6) $$$$
California

Down a romantic lane leading to warm dining rooms within historic brick walls, Hawthorne Lane prepares a California-Asian fusion with precision. Roasted beef carpaccio, grilled venison and seared miso glazed scallops are business account pleasers. Reservations essential.

☎ 777-9779 ✉ 22 Hawthorne Ln ⏰ 11:30am-2pm & 5:30-10pm Mon-Thu, to 10:30pm Fri, 5:30-10:30pm Sat Ⓜ Montgomery St 🚌 10, 15 Ⓥ ♿

Red's Java House (5, F6) $
Burgers

Just a little shack squatting beside an old wharf, Red's is tops with the construction crews who order the famous

Head to the Ferry Building Marketplace for brunch

double cheeseburger and a Bud in a bottle. Cash only.
☎ 777-5626 ✉ Pier 30, Embarcadero ⏱ 6am-4pm Mon-Tue, to 8pm Wed-Fri, 9am-3pm Sat & Sun 🚋 F line 🚲 ♿

Slanted Door (5, E4) $$
Vietnamese fusion

Vietnam's light and refreshing cuisine, which includes inheritances from France and China, has met a kindred mate in California's bountiful latitude. Modern and exciting, Slanted Door is a long-running favorite with its *jicama* and grapefruit salad and shaking beef. A Mission location (4, B2; 584 Valencia St) does Vietnamese street food. Reservations essential for dinner.
☎ 861-8032 ✉ 1 Ferry Bldg, Embarcadero & Market St ⏱ 11:30am-2:30pm & 5:30-10pm Ⓜ Embarcadero 🚋 F line ⛴ Blue & Gold and Golden Gate from Tiburon, Sausalito, Oakland & Alameda 🅿 Pier 1/2 & Washington-Embarcadero lots Ⓥ ♿

Tú Lan Restaurant (5, B7) $
Vietnamese

The wage slave's version of a power lunch, Tú Lan does tasty, waistline busting Vietnamese food. Try #17 (imperial rolls, rice noodles and pork kebabs) to induce the 3pm office coma. Although Tú Lan's is the kitchen version of the surrounding flophouses, the efficient and pleasant staff will make you feel like middle management.
☎ 626-0927 ✉ 8 6th St ⏱ 11am-9:30pm Mon-Sat Ⓜ Civic Center 🚋 F line, 9, 19 🚲 Ⓥ ♿

Waterfront Restaurant & Café (5, D3) $$$
California

Usually the better the view, the worse the food. The Waterfront is an exception. Whether you're eating in the casual café downstairs or the restaurant above, the fresh fish on your plate will compete for attention with the bay and the boats out the windows.
☎ 391-2696 ✉ Pier 7, Embarcadero & Broadway ⏱ 11am-11pm 🚋 F line, 12 Ⓥ ♿

Yank Sing (5, E4) $$$
Chinese

Think dim sum is just a salty hangover cure for wannabe food adventurers? Yank Sing will set you on the gourmet path with little lettuce cups filled with minced squab, deep-fried crab claws and luscious Peking duck. There is another branch at 49 Stevenson St (5, C5; ☎ 541-4949).
☎ 957-9300 ⏱ 11am-3pm ✉ 1 Rincon Center, 101 Spear St Ⓜ Embarcadero 🚋 1, 2, 9, 14, 21 🚲 Ⓥ ♿

Worth the Trip

Chez Panisse (7, C1; ☎ 510-548-5525; 1517 Shattuck Ave, Berkeley; ⏱ 6pm & 8:30pm Mon-Sat; BART Downtown Berkeley) If California cuisine has a home, this is it. The converted Arts and Crafts style house is fittingly dressed down for the honest but intense flavors of Alice Water's food revolution. Make reservations months in advance, or try the upstairs café (⏱ 11:30am-3pm & 5-10:30pm Mon-Sat), which is more flexible, but not as luxurious.

Roxanne's (☎ 924-5004; 320 Magnolia Ave, Larkspur; ⏱ 5:30-10pm Tue-Sat; 101 north to Tamalpais Rd exit to Larkspur) Welcome to an innovative concept – haute cuisine for the raw food movement. Believers claim they can taste all the healthy nutrients with just one bite, while skeptics grumble that it should cost less if nothing is cooked. Everyone is in agreement that California is nuts. Worth a trip for the curious.

French Laundry (1, A2; ☎ 707-944-2380; 6640 Washington St, Yountville; ⏱ 5:30-9:30pm Mon-Fri, 11am-1pm & 5:30-9:30pm Sat & Sun) Considered one of the best restaurants in the country, French Laundry is chef-owner Thomas Keller's exquisite and romantic indulgence. Set in a stone cottage, formerly a steam laundry, the restaurant fills up quick; make reservations months in advance.

Entertainment

There are just a few simple rules for doing San Francisco nightlife. First, you don't need the weekend as an excuse to rock out; any day will do thanks to the rotating coronation of arbitrary days in the middle of the week as the 'new' Friday. Second, follow the lead of full-time San Franciscans and use your nighttime bar crawl as a fashion catwalk. This city doesn't dress up like New York or Los Angeles, it 'plays' dress up with recycled period costumes or flamboyant couture (more Chloe Sevigny than Sarah Jessica Parker). Whatever look you go for, avoid predictable (too Marina) or stuffy (too Financial District).

What's Going On
San Franciscans start planning their weekend at around 9am on the preceding Monday, and there are many sources to which they turn. Free weeklies such as the *Bay Guardian* (www.sfbg.com) and the *SF Weekly* (www.sfweekly.com) list current entertainment events, as does the *San Francisco Chronicle* (www.sfgate. com). An invaluable online resource for alternative arts events listed by venue or organization is www.laugh ingsquid.org.

Now you're ready to hit the town. The cultural performances, such as the opera and ballet, revolve around the Civic Center and Hayes Valley, where wining and dining serve as evening preludes. Hipsters throng the strip of bars along the Valencia St corridor, which exudes a knee-deep art school vibe. Constantly changing is the latest 'in' club peddling the most recent incarnation of the cosmopolitan, mojito or sake-tini for pretties who skip dinner and don't like beer. The center of the dance club scene is South of Market (SoMa) with its mix of straight and gay places. And rest assured that as an out-of-towner, you'll start and finish at least one night at the bars (and maybe a strip club) in North Beach.

Even with all of these options, San Francisco isn't an all night town. Folks stagger off to bed before the wee hours in readiness for early morning bike rides or yoga classes. Most bars close without protest at 2am.

The US drinking age of 21 years old is ardently enforced and an ID to prove it is required to enter most bars. California's bars have been smoke-free since 1998 to protect the health of restaurant and bar workers. Most bars provide ashtrays outside or on an outdoor patio.

The band Sidestepper playing at the annual Stern Grove Festival

Special Events

January *Dine About Town* – month-long; San Francisco's top restaurants offer phenomenal fixed price lunch and dinner menus
Chinese New Year – the Golden Dragon Parade rolls through downtown late January or early February

February *Independent Film Festival* – early February; emerging low-budget masterpieces are screened at different theaters in the city
Noise Pop – late February; local and national alt-rock bands plug in for a week-long festival

March *St Patrick's Day* – mid-March; Irish Americans and friends march down Market St and refresh themselves all around town

April *Cherry Blossom Festival* – late April; martial arts, dancing and other events in Japantown
International Film Festival – late April to early May; two weeks of international films from over 45 countries

May *Bay to Breakers* – third Sunday; 100,000 runners in wacky costumes, including birthday suits, do the 7 miles from the Embarcadero to Ocean Beach
Carnaval – Memorial Day weekend; dancers, floats and samba bands parade down Mission St in honor of Fat Tuesday

June *Pride Parade* – last Sunday; up to a half-million marchers and spectators celebrate gay pride
North Beach Street Fair – mid-June; Italian food, street music and a swing-dancing priest
Haight St Fair – mid-June; 'special' brownies, music and lots of patchouli at this hippie street fair

July *Independence Day* – July 4; fireworks (which are usually obscured by fog) are launched over the Bay

September *Fringe Festival* – early September; marathon run of comedy, solo and alternative performances at discount prices
Opera in the Park – first Sunday following the start of opera season; free show at Sharon Meadow in Golden Gate Park
San Francisco Blues Festival – mid- to late September; two days of blues on the Great Meadow at Fort Mason
Folsom St Fair – late September; tens of thousands of leather folk and voyeuristic average folk converge for a benefit street fair

October *Castro St Fair* – first weekend; arts and crafts, music and food, masses of gays and lesbians
Jazz Festival – late October to early November; performances in venues all around town
Halloween – October 31; the city dresses up from morning to night, crowds converge on the Castro to gawk and parade

BARS & PUBS

Buena Vista Café (5, A2)
Claiming to have invented Irish coffee, this pub and café is the only place worth a damn in the whole tourist ghetto of Fisherman's Wharf. Unscientific figures claim that bartenders serve over 2000 glasses of the stuff every day – an astounding number considering the slow service.
☎ 474-5044 ✉ 2765 Hyde St ☺ 9am-2am Mon-Fri, 8am-2am Sat & Sun 🚋 Powell-Hyde cable car, 10, 19, 30, 47 ♿

Locals enjoying a quiet beer at one of the city's many pubs

C Bobby's Owl Tree (5, B5)
A free drink is awarded if you're able to correctly guess the number of owl motifs that occupy this rat pack-esque bar. Careful though, the owner is notoriously moody. You're safer in a cozy swivel chair where an aproned bartender will bring you drinks (a stiff Manhattan perhaps) and bar snacks with accompanying moist towellettes. Remember, clean hands maketh the man.
☎ 776-9344 ✉ 601 Post St ☺ 5pm-2am Wed-Sat 🚋 Powell-Mason & Powell-Hyde cable car, 2, 3, 4 ♿

Delirium (4, B2) The coiffed and the don't cares form an uneasy nighttime zoo along 16th St's watering hole wonderland. A little too seedy-looking for the much maligned yuppies, Delirium (formerly known as Albion) is a straight up dive bar with a solid jukebox, friendly bartenders and

Chimay on tap. In the back room, DJs play an eclectic mix of dance tunes.
☎ 552-5525 ✉ 3139 16th St ☺ 2pm-2am Ⓜ 16th St 🚌 22, 26 ♿

Doc's Clock (4, C3) Lit by magenta neon, this dive bar takes on a classic hue when the bar stools are sparsely populated by tattooed Mission locals. In the far back, the quirky house band does a chameleon-quick change from Hawaiian ukulele

tributes some nights to jazz ensembles other nights.
☎ 824-3627 ✉ 2575 Mission St ☺ 4pm-2am Mon-Fri, 6pm-2am Sat, 8pm-2am Sun 🚌 14, 49 ♿

Gold Dust (5, C6) Quite possibly the best tourist bar ever invented, the Gold Dust does a convincing version of a Gold Rush saloon with rich tapestries, a handsome wooden bar and unflappable bartenders. The nightly band rambles from drinking

The Tamale Lady
When the night gets blurry and the shirt gets dribbled with beer, that is when the Tamale Lady makes her rounds through the Mission bars. More prolific than visions of the Virgin Mary, the Tamale Lady appears just when hunger might be disastrously sated with another round. From table to table, she dispenses her homemade cornmeal creations (beef, chicken and veggie) from a round cooler for only $2 apiece. Regulars can smell her coming down the street and are so thankful for her service that they recently organized a 50th birthday party in her honor, complete with bumper stickers that say 'I Love the Tamale Lady' and a documentary about her life.

tunes to string jigs, and requests are gladly accepted by talking to 'Fillup the jar.' If you need to step out to smoke, ask for a humorous seat-saver card.

☎ 397-1695 ✉ 247 Powell St ☽ 6am-2am Ⓜ Powell St 🚌 Powell-Hyde & Powell-Mason cable car, F line ♿

Hayes & Vine Wine Bar (6, C5) A mouth-watering menu of wine and hors d'oeuvres gives you a good excuse for salivating at a bar. This crisp space cradles pre-theatergoers, dinks (double income no kids) as well as an older singles scene.

☎ 626-5301 ✉ 377 Hayes St ☽ 5pm-midnight Mon-Thu, to 1am Fri & Sat, to 10pm Sun 🚌 F line, 21 ♿

Gordon Biersch (5, E5) On a sunny day, Gordon Biersch's outdoor patio, with a view of the Bay Bridge, reels in cloistered cubicle dwellers for a post-work pint-tossing session. Tasty microbrews, as well as beer-battered snacks and burgers keep the old Hills Bros coffee plant filled when the weather turns melancholy. All ages welcome.

☎ 243-8246 ✉ 2 Harrison St ☽ 11:30am-11pm Sun-Tue, to midnight Wed & Thu, to 1am Fri & Sat 🚌 F line, 12 ♿

La Rondalla (4, C3) This margarita cantina always feels like a New Year's Eve celebration. Every inch is festooned with twinkling lights and tinsel. Mariachis,

stuffed like tamales into their black suits, serenade the crowd along the serpentine bar. Forget about those fishbowl fakers at Chi-Chis, these margaritas are the size of a shot glass and stiffer than rigor mortis. All ages welcome in the restaurant.

☎ 647-7474 ✉ 901 Valencia St ☽ 5pm-midnight Sun-Thu, to 3am Fri & Sat 🚌 22, 26 ♿

Lion's Pub (6, A3) This classy corner bar should serve as a paradigm for all of Pacific Heights – good drinks, no prowlers and not a single tropical shirt. Perhaps the veil of plants, making it look like a gay bar, keeps out the neighborhood's cliquish breeders. Inside a jungle of potted plants mixes with a ski lodge aesthetic, a stone fireplace and relaxed imbibers sporting a post-adrenaline glow. All of the drinks are made with fresh fruit juices and the happy hour spread (brie, smoked salmon and artichoke dip) rivals some

wedding banquets.

☎ 567-6565 ✉ 2062 Divisadero St ☽ 4pm-2am 🚌 1, 24 ♿

Li Po's (5, C4) Looking like a Chinese temple, Li Po's reputation as a hang-out for Chinese mobsters fuels a steady diet of average White kids overdosed on Bruce Lee movies. If the night is slow, patrons play the ubiquitous Chinatown bar game of dice.

☎ 982-0072 ✉ 916 Grant Ave ☽ 2pm-2am 🚌 Powell-Mason & Powell-Hyde cable car, 30 ♿

Noc Noc (6, B5) This cavernous dive bar is what Fred and Wilma Flintstone's place might look like if they were Haight hippies not prehistoric suburbanites. A drum-and-bass soundtrack accompanies a reputable beer selection and a barely legal crowd.

☎ 861-5811 ✉ 557 Haight St ☽ 5pm-2am 🚌 6, 7, 22, 71 ♿

Activists of the Cloth

In a town of dogmatic convictions, the Sisters of Perpetual Indulgence, a unique and heretical order of gay men, use humor to raise awareness and funds for gay issues and charities. Their history can be traced back to a legitimate convent in Cedar Rapids, Iowa, who lent a San Francisco production of the *Sound of Music* some retired habits. The habits came out of the closet three years later and the Sisters were born. Making theatric appearances at any public gathering, the Sisters are hard to miss with their French wimple habits, kabuki makeup and such divinely inspired names as Sister Missionary Position and Sister Phyllis Stein. For an upcoming calendar of events, visit www.thesisters.org.

**Plough and the Stars
(2, E1)** This is about as close to an Irish working guy's pub as you'll find in the city. People with real brogues share a drink after work or in lieu of dinner (if it was good enough for nursing mothers...) There's Irish music six nights a week, and even step dancing from time to time.
☎ 751-1122 ✉ 116 Clement St ◷ 4pm-2am Mon-Thu, noon-2am Fri-Sun 🚌 2 ♿

Redwood Room (5, B6)
Panelled in the ruby wood of one entire sequoia tree, this post-Prohibition bar has been updated with etched Venetian glass tables, cocktails of Cuban persuasions and New York elitism. An after work splurge morphs into a weekend glamour contest complete with a discriminating door policy and celebrity sightings. Go before 9pm to get in.
☎ 775-4700 ✉ 495 Geary St, Clift Hotel ◷ 5pm-2am Ⓜ Powell St 🚌 38 ♿

Saloon (5, C3) San Francisco's oldest beer joint started life as a fruit market in 1858 with a side venture in Christmas ornaments, until the owner realized that the holiday came only once a year but happy hour was every day. The resulting saloon survived the 1906 earthquake and fickle drinking trends with possibly the same coat of paint.
☎ 989-7666 ✉ 1232 Grant Ave ◷ noon-2am 🚌 15, 30, 41 ♿

Saloon, a 1906 quake survivor and still going strong

Spec's (5, C3) Down an alley beside Tosca's Café, Spec's reflects its pedigree as a seafarers' bar with a cluttered collection of memorabilia from distant ports. The crowd is an equally well traveled mix, all engaged in swashbuckling tales of office life. Reigning passively from a spot-lit corner is a portrait of Julia, the owner's dearly departed spouse.
☎ 421-4112 ✉ 12 William Saroyan Place ◷ 4:30pm-2am Mon-Fri, 5:30pm-2am Sat & Sun 🚌 15, 30, 41 ♿

Tonga Room (5, B5)
This bar is a little bit of Waikiki on the top of Nob Hill. Tropical music, a choice of tropical drinks and even tropical rainstorms complete with lightning and thunder are all here for the price of a drink and a modest cover charge in the evenings when the floating band is on duty.
☎ 772-5278 ✉ 950 Mason St, bottom of the Fairmont hotel 💲 cover $3 ◷ 5pm-2am, shows 8pm nightly 🚌 California St, Powell-Mason & Powell-Hyde cable cars, 1 ♿

Toronado (6, B5) While San Francisco wine connoisseurs imbibe amid versions of Tuscany, beer aficionados prefer roadhouses. The shoulder line up here is nearly 100% dudes, more precisely disgruntled bookstore clerks nodding along to speed metal and massaging tall pints from the best breweries in Belgium, Germany and California.
☎ 863-2276 ✉ 547 Haight St ◷ 11:30am-2am 🚌 J line, 6, 7, 22, 71 ♿

Tosca Café (5, C3) Come on through the art deco door, have a seat at the mahogany bar and order a house cappuccino from the crisp white-clad bartender. Your drink will have steamed milk, Ghirardelli chocolate and brandy. If you have a spare quarter, throw it in the jukebox and pick from a wide selection of opera classics. Your next drink could be a handsome negroni or just a plain old Budweiser – both would be welcomed in this egalitarian holdout.
☎ 391-1244 ✉ 242 Columbus Ave ◷ 5pm-2am Tue-Sat 🚌 15, 41, 45 ♿

On the Town Alone

No need to sit around your hotel room alone watching a movie on Lifetime. Single tickets to performances are often easier to find than tickets for two or three people (just show up early; there's usually someone with an extra ticket to sell). For drinking and lounging, San Franciscans are as outgoing at night as they are during the day. Find yourself a bar stool at **Zam Zam** (below), **Tosca Café** (p83) or the **Hayes & Vine Wine Bar** (p82), and before your second round you'll be swapping tales with a talker.

Vesuvio Café (5, C3) Hep cats and cool chicks once rapped and rhymed in this famous Beatnik bar. These days bookworms and well-worn locals camp out in the nooks and crannies, and a steady supply of tourists gawk at (or even pose beside) the bar's historic photos of literary legends. ☎ 362-3370 ✉ 255 Columbus Ave 🕒 6am-2am 🚌 15, 41, 45 ♿

Zam Zam (2, F2) With Persian-inspired murals, arched doorways and carved wooden screens, Zam Zam is a convivial retreat for the burned out, dive bar imbibers. The horseshoe-shaped bar invites audible conversation over the sounds of Chet Baker and Ella Fitzgerald. ☎ 861-2545 ✉ 1633 Haight St 🕒 3pm-2am 🚌 6, 7, 43, 71 ♿

Zeitgeist (4, B1) Zeitgeist's belching siren call is irresistible on a fogless night. In the backyard beer garden, bikers, bike messengers and sensible shoe wearers join a collective push to get loaded as the barbecue pit wafts smoke over the crowd. Zeitgeist has great microbrews and cocktails. ☎ 255-7505 ✉ 199 Valencia St 🕒 9am-2am 🚌 F line, 14, 26, 49 ♿

A famous Beatnik bar, the Vesuvio Café still draws a crowd of bookworms

COFFEEHOUSES

Atlas Café (3, E4) Slackers and endangered dot-commies hang out in the sunny back patio or catch a Thursday bluegrass jam. The songs of Appalachia may seem out of place when sitting beside a punked-out lesbian couple, but the tunes of rivers and railroads were imported to California by silver miners long before revivalism became vogue. ☎ 648-1047 ✉ 3049 20th St at Alabama St $ no cover ⏰ 7am-10pm Mon-Fri, 8am-10pm Sat, 8am-8pm Sun, music

8-10pm Thu & 4-7pm Sat 🚌 9, 27 ♿

Brainwash (5, B8) There are other places to get an espresso or sandwich while you do your wash, but there aren't many that also have live performances. Spoken word, poetry slams, comedy and music fill a weekly calendar. ☎ 431-9274 ✉ www .brainwash.com ✉ 1122 Folsom St $ no cover ⏰ 7:30am-11pm Sun-Thu, to midnight Fri & Sat 🚌 12, 19 ♿

Canvas Gallery, Café & Lounge (2, D3) This low-key café has imported art-for-the-masses to the sleepy Inner Sunset. Jazz trios, rotating exhibits, local artisan fairs and improv nights – the talent is here and so are the fancy cocktails, but none of the 'tude has followed. ☎ 504-0060 ✉ www .thecanvasgallery.com ✉ 1200 9th Ave $ no cover ⏰ 7am-midnight Mon-Fri, 8am-midnight Sat & Sun 🚌 29, 44, 71 ♿

DANCE CLUBS

111 Minna (5, D5) San Francisco's retro romance is in full effect at this hip industrial space that offers a mellow mood for post-work unwinding. Gallery shows, film screenings and four nights of DJs mix art, music and hedonism into a stylish goulash. ☎ 974-1719 ✉ www .111minnagallery com ✉ 111 Minna St $ cover varies ⏰ bar 5pm-2am Mon-Sat, gallery noon-5pm Mon-Fri Ⓜ Montgomery St 🚌 5, 6, 7, 14, 21, 71 ♿

1015 Folsom St (5, C7) A co-ed bathhouse in the 1970s, 1015 Folsom St honors international DJs in its main dance hall with off-shoot rooms for a different scene. The crowd is diverse and the sound system strong enough to clean your clothes.

Be prepared for a pat-down before you enter (there's a serious no-drugs policy after some problems with the SFPD). ☎ 431-1200 ✉ www .1015.com ✉ 1015 Folsom St $ cover $10+ ⏰ 10pm-6am Thu-Sun (hours may vary with events) 🚌 12, 27 ♿

Endup (5, C7) This South of Market institution illustrates San Francisco in all its polymorphous sexuality.

Thursdays are for techno-heads, and self-explanatory Fag Fridays stumble into the Saturday 'after hours' party starting at 6am. The Sunday T-dance is a daylong revival at the church of St Endup. ☎ 646-0999 ✉ www .theendup.com ✉ 401 6th St $ cover $10+ ⏰ 10pm-4:30am Thu, 10pm-6am Fri, 6am-4pm & 10pm-4am Sat, 6am-8pm & 10pm-4am Sun 🚌 12, 27 ♿

All-hours parties make the Endup a SoMa institution

Guide to the SF Sound

San Francisco left its greatest impression on the national music scene with the psychedelic rock of the 1960s. But inside the city limits, the young ones hardly pay homage to those classic rock days; instead they revolve around the urban music scene that unites New York, London and Chicago.

Electronica – Born in the UK, modern DJ dance culture emigrated to the US via underground raves and specialty record stores. In the mid-1990s, San Francisco emerged as the stateside outpost of the scene's subgenre of drum-and-bass (jungle). At its peak, the Lower Haight was an electronica universe inspiringso many enthusiasts that the city claimed more DJs than dance floors. With the sunken economy, the number of amateur spinners have declined, but the dance scene lives on. Spundae Records hosts Friday night raves at **1015 Folsom** (p85), and drum-and-bass DJs frequently spin at **The Top** (opposite). **Stompy** (www.stompy.com) is an annual West Coast dance party held at different venues in the city.

Turntablism – Tracing its roots to rap and hip-hop, turntablism rotates the spotlight on the DJs rather than the emcees. Instead of dance mixes, turntablists scratch, mix and challenge other DJs to match skills. Part spectacle and part musicianship, the scene was best epitomized by the Invisbl Skratch Piklz, a Bay Area group of freestyle DJs whose founding members (including QBert and Mix Master Mike) have gone on to successful solo careers. At clubs like **Milk** (opposite), freestylists usually appear side by side with hip-hop acts; look for shows hosted by **Future Primitive** (www.futureprimitivesound.com), a San Francisco–based record label.

Indie Rock – For the classicists, guitar rock still rules the city's dingy clubs and collective soundtrack. Splintered into a million subgenres, the indie scene can be poorly described as a motley crew of post-punk, post-metal, noise pop, garage bands. Clubs such as **Café du Nord** (p88) and **Bottom of the Hill** (p88) feature a lot of indie acts and the annual **Noise Pop Festival** (www.noisepop.com) draws out locals, including Boyskout and Low Flying Owls.

Harry Denton's Starlight Room (5, C5) This is the place to go when you want to feel like a glamourpuss from a black-and-white movie. Overlooking Union Square high atop the Drake Hotel, as they used to say on the radio, it's dressy, pricey and worth a signature martini and a fox-trot around the dance floor.
☎ 395-8595
🖳 www.harrydenton.com
✉ 450 Powell St, Sir Francis Drake Hotel 💲 cover varies 🕒 4:30pm-2am
Ⓜ Powell St 🚃 Powell-Hyde & Powell-Mason cable cars, 2, 3, 4 ♿

Metronome Ballroom (3, E4) If you've had enough with dancing solo, try the revived art of partnering from swing to salsa at this spacious ballroom on Friday, Saturday and Sunday nights. Lessons are offered to get beginners up to speed with the devotees. All ages.
☎ 252-9000 🖳 www.metronomeballroom.com
✉ 1830 17th St
💲 cover $8-15
🕒 dance party hours vary 🚍 9, 22 ♿

Milk (2, E2) The Upper Haight was not a destination for booty-shaking, well, not until it got Milk. This chic club of retro interiors is heavy on hip-hop and periodic turntable showdowns.

Sushi Sundays feature four free bands plus à la carte sushi.
☎ 387-6455
🖳 www.milksf.com
✉ 1840 Haight St
💲 cover $3-10 🕒 hours vary 🚍 N line, 6, 7, 33, 43, 66, 71 ♿

Top (6, B5) One of the best small clubs for San Francisco's electronica scene, the Top consistently spins out drum-and-bass heavies throughout the week. Lots of sweaty bodies, no décor and no attitude.
☎ 864-7386
✉ 424 Haight St
💲 cover $5-10
🕒 5pm-2am
🚍 6, 22, 71 ♿

CINEMAS

Castro Theatre (4, A1) Too big to call an 'art house,' but far too arty to be a movie theater, the Castro is a survivor from the days of movie palaces. Mosaic tiles, a huge billboard marquee and art deco interiors adorn this grand dame, which now shows classic and art films. Before the main feature, a Wurlitzer organ appears out of the stage for a previewing performance and a finale of 'San Francisco.'
☎ 621-6120 🖳 www.thecastrotheatre.com
✉ 429 Castro St
💲 $8.50/5.50
🚍 K, L, M lines to Castro, F line, 24, 35, 37 ♿

Metreon (5, C6) This is the behemoth of 4th St. There are 18 screens, including an IMAX, almost enough to fill the five-story garage across the street on a rainy day. See a Hollywood flick and have a bite in the food court.
☎ 369-6000
🖳 www.metreon.com
✉ 101 4th St
💲 $10/6.75 Ⓜ Powell St
🚍 14, 15, 30 ♿

Red Vic Movie House (2, F2) A worker-owned collective, the Red Vic is an art house poster child – sofas instead of chairs, popcorn with brewer's yeast, and tea served in mugs. The selections are cult classics, independents and documentaries (often with a Bay Area bent).
☎ 668-3994 🖳 www.redvicmoviehouse.com
✉ 1727 Haight St
💲 $4/7 🚍 N line, 6, 7, 43, 71 ♿

Roxie (4, B2) The Mission's local art house, Roxie shows French classics, American underground flicks and lots of documentaries.
☎ 863-1087 🖳 www.roxie.com ✉ 3117 16th St 💲 $8/4 Ⓜ 16th St
🚍 22, 26, 49 ♿

Catch a classic flick at the art deco Castro Theatre

JAZZ, BLUES & ROCK

Bill Graham Civic Auditorium (5, A7) This 5000-seat auditorium fills that gap between a music hall and an arena. The Civic Auditorium has hosted everything from the San Francisco Opera to the Grateful Dead, who used to play here every New Year's Eve.
☎ 974-4000 ▢ www .billgrahamcivic.com ✉ 99 Grove St Ⓜ Civic Center 🚌 9, 19, 21, 26 ♿

Bimbo's 365 (5, A2) This old-fashioned nightclub has adapted to the times over and over. Rita Hayworth danced in the chorus line here, but today you'll be going to see more modern performances ranging from rock to jazz.
☎ 474-0365 ▢ www .bimbos365club.com ✉ 1025 Columbus Ave

box office 10am-4pm Mon-Fri 🚋 Powell-Mason cable car, 15, 30 ♿

Boom Boom Room (6, B4) The Room has been booming with the sounds of rhythm and blues and juke jiving since the early days of when the Fillmore was the nightclub strip of this African American neighborhood. The Room has held on to its location and reputation even as the neighborhood shifted demographics.
☎ 673-8000 ▢ www .boomboomblues.com ✉ 1601 Fillmore St ☽ 4pm-2am, shows start 9pm 🚌 22, 38 ♿

Bottom of the Hill (3, F4) At the base of Potrero Hill, every up-and-coming band worth their feedback have played at this bare-bones

club. Nightly shows feature alternative, rock-a-billy, and punk bands earning the Hill its *Rolling Stone* magazine title of San Francisco's best place for live music.
☎ 621-4455 ▢ www .bottomofthehill.com ✉ 1233 17th St at Missouri St ☽ 8:30pm-2am Sat-Thu, 3pm-2am Fri 🚌 19, 22 ♿

Café du Nord (4, B1) This former speakeasy of red velvet interiors indulges San Franciscans in the aesthetics of the city's beloved Victorian past. Beyond the aging recipe of a cocktail lounge, Café du Nord adds a modern twist with a weekly roster of must-see local music.
☎ 861-5016 ▢ www .cafedunord.com ✉ 2170 Market St ☽ 1hr before showtime, 6pm-2am Fri 🚋 K, L, M lines to Castro, 22, 37 ♿ no

Fillmore (6, B4) Since Bill Graham put on a benefit for the San Francisco Mime Troupe featuring Jefferson Airplane on February 4, 1966, the Fillmore has hosted all the names of acid rock and most of the other names of rock that followed. All ages for most shows.
☎ 346-6000 ▢ www .thefillmore.com ✉ 1805 Geary Blvd ☽ show nights 7:30-10pm Mon-Sat, 10am-4pm Sun 🚌 22, 38 ♿

Great American Music Hall (5, A6) One of the best venues for mid-sized shows, the Great American

The cut glass interior of Bimbo's 365

Music Hall has a stage-level standing room, upstairs balcony seating and good acoustics. All ages for most shows.
☎ 885-0750
🖥 www.gamh.com
✉ 859 O'Farrell St
🕐 box office 10am-4pm Sun-Mon, noon-6pm Tue-Sat, to 9pm show nights
🚌 19, 38 ♿

Pier 23 Café (5, D2) Rolex Rollers, not the Hell's Angels, congregate at this bayfront shack for live music, ranging from jazz to R&B, on most evenings and weekends. There are also free salsa lessons on Wednesday.
☎ 362-5125
🖥 www.pier23cafe.com
✉ Pier 23, Embarcadero
🕐 showtimes usually 5pm or 10pm
🚌 F line ♿

Slim's (5, B9) This brand-name club on SoMa's 11th St strip is partly owned by Boz Scaggs, who lives up the hill in Pacific Heights. Originally a blues club, it features singer-songwriters, rock acts and a smattering of soul and blues groups. All ages for most shows.
☎ 255-0333
🖥 www.slims-sf.com
✉ 333 11th St 🕐 box office 10:30am-6pm Mon-Fri 🚌 9, 12, 47 ♿

Warfield (5, B6) This old vaudeville theater is managed by the Bill Graham organization and presents national acts that prefer not to play to a super coliseum. Here you can experience the sounds of the present with the conveniences

Rhythm and blues keep the Boom Boom Room jiving

of the past, including a restaurant and bar. All ages for most shows.
☎ 775-7722 ✉ 982 Market St 🕐 box office at the Fillmore 10am-4pm Sun, show nights 7:30-10pm Ⓜ Civic Center 🚌 5, 6, 7, 21, 66, 71 ♿

Yoshi's (7, B6) Though no one likes to admit it, San Francisco has been jilted by jazz joints. To see the legends, you have to cross the bay to Yoshi's, a Japanese restaurant in Oakland. The

well-dressed space puts the prim audience close enough to smell McCoy Tyner's cologne.
☎ 510-238-9200
🖥 www.yoshis.com
✉ 510 Embarcadero West, Oakland 🕐 8pm & 10pm Mon-Sat, 7pm & 9pm Sun Ⓜ 12th St 🚌 Bay Bridge to I-880 south to Broadway-Alameda exit, right on 5th St, follow signs for Jack London Sq ⚓ Blue and Gold Fleet Ferries Oakland-Alameda ♿

Uber Coliseums

Diminutive San Francisco has to look beyond its borders for performance spaces big enough for the Rolling Stones and huge touring festivals. The really big, big shows are held at the indoor arena at the **Oakland Coliseum** (☎ 510-569-2121; I-880 at Hegenberger Rd) or outdoors at the **Shoreline Amphitheater** (☎ 650-967-3000; off Hwy 101 in Mountain View), or the **Chronicle Pavilion** (☎ 925-363-5701; 2200 Kirker Pass Rd, Concord).

THEATER & COMEDY

American Conservatory Theater (5, B6) San Francisco's premier theater company is based at the Geary Theater. It's a stage for classics, revivals and new work by the likes of Tom Stoppard. The school here was a training ground for Danny Glover, Annette Bening and Denzel Washington. ☎ 749-2228 💻 www .act-sfbay.org ✉ 415 Geary St, box office 405 Geary St 💲 prices vary ⏰ box office noon-6pm or noon-showtime Ⓜ Powell St 🚃 Powell-Hyde & Powell-Mason cable cars, 2, 3, 4, 38 ♿

Bay Area Theatersports (6, B1) BATS has tried to improve the improv business by turning it into a team sport. Two teams compete over a series of scenes and challenges. Three judges award points and determine who is the winner. You judge for yourself. ☎ 474-8935 💻 www.improv.org ✉ Fort Mason Center, Bldg B, 3rd fl 💲 $8-12 ⏰ 8pm Thu-Sun 🚌 22, 30 🅿 free ♿

CELLspace (3, E4) In the artist bohemia of the Mission, CELLspace (Collectively Explorative Learning Lab) is a volunteer-run warehouse that hosts puppet shows, drop-in breakdancing classes and other offbeat endeavors. The affiliated studio provides work space for artists preparing sculptures for the Burning Man festival or floats for the Carnaval festival; the curious are welcome to peer in. ☎ 648-7562 💻 www.cellspace.org ✉ 2050 Bryant St 💲 $5-10 ⏰ showtimes vary 🚌 27 ♿

Exit Theater (5, B6) Touted as the best (3000 miles) Off Broadway theater, Exit hosts independent shows by various small-scale theater companies in a setting so intimate you can see them sweat. It also organizes the annual San Francisco Fringe Festival (p80). ☎ 673-3847 💻 www.sffringe.org ✉ 156 Eddy St 💲 $15-20 ⏰ box office 30min before shows Ⓜ Civic Center 🚌 F line, 5 ♿

Actors of the future hone their craft at the American Conservatory Theater

Magic Theater (6, B1)
Sam Shepard put the Magic on the map when he was resident playwright here, before Jessica Lange and the movies. It's still the kind of place Sam Shepard would work, two tiny spaces seating about 160 people apiece, showing new work by both established and not-so-established writers.
☎ 441-8822 ✉ **Fort Mason Center, Bldg D** ☽ box office noon-5pm Tue-Sat 🚌 22, 30 ♿

New Conservatory Theater (4, C5) The NCT presents work by young playwrights and old standards from under-served voices, including the popular Pride Season.
☎ 861-8972 🖳 www .nctcsf.org ✉ 25 Van Ness Ave ☽ box office

1:30-7pm Tue-Sat 🚌 K, L, M, N lines to Van Ness, F line, 21 ♿

Project Artaud Theater (3, E4) Edgy and innovative, Theater Artaud is the place to see performance artists, dancers or artists such as the Kronos Quartet. It started out in 1972 as beyond fringe and has matured into off-beat sophistication.
☎ 626-4370 🖳 www .artaud.org ✉ 450 Florida St ☽ box office 1-4pm Tue-Sat 🚌 12, 22, 27 ♿

Punch Line (5, D4) The top comedy club in the city, this is where Margaret Cho plays when she comes home. Intimate surroundings with good sight lines exposes you to the comics'

witty observations. This is an 18+ venue.
☎ 397-7573 🖳 www .punchlinecomedyclub .com ✉ 444 Battery St 💲 $7.50-40, 2 drink min ☽ box office 7:30pm, phone reservations 1-6pm Ⓜ Embarcadero 🚌 1, 10, 41 ♿

San Francisco Mime Troupe (4, B2) The ACT of the left, the Mime Troupe is the premier guerrilla theater company of the city. Expect political musical theater, half Irving Berlin, half *commedia dell'arte*, served up for free in Mission Dolores Park and other parks every summer since the 1960s.
☎ 285-1720 🖳 www.sfmt.org ✉ Mission Dolores Park, at 18th St ☽ schedule varies 🚌 J line, 33 ♿

CLASSICAL MUSIC, OPERA & DANCE

Audium (6, C3) A more mature version of a Pink Floyd lightshow, composer Stan Shaff presents his sound sculptures in a dark-ened theater where listeners sitting in concentric circles 'see' the sounds moving

through space. Emerging from 169 speakers located in the walls, floor and ceiling, the sounds are choreo-graphed through their intensity and frequency.
☎ 771-1616 🖳 www.audium.org

✉ 1616 Bush St 💲 $12 ☽ shows 8:30pm Fri & Sat, box office from 8pm 🚌 2, 3, 4, 47, 49 ♿

Herbst Theatre (5, A7) The Herbst is a stately yet intimate theater hosting a spectrum of cultural programs, including classical music concerts and dance performances. The ac-claimed City Arts & Lectures, a conversation series with influential writers and thinkers, is held here annually.
☎ 554-6315 🖳 www .performances.org ✉ 401 Van Ness Ave ☽ box office 1hr before performances

Stern Grove Freebies
On Sundays in the summer, San Francisco's cultural performances are released from the sterile music halls into a lush canyon of redwoods and eucalyptus. Bring a blanket and a picnic to enjoy the symphony, opera, ballet or pop music from the likes of Eddie Palmieri or Les Yeux Noir, and it's all for free. **Stern Grove** (3, B5; ☎ 252-6252; www.sterngrove.org) is at the corner of 19th Ave and Sloat Blvd. Arrive early and bring lots of layers in case the fog rolls in.

Ⓜ Civic Center 🚆 K, L, M lines to Van Ness, F line, 5, 21, 47, 49 ♿

San Francisco Ballet
(5, A7) One of the oldest ballet companies in the US, it presents its repertory season at the Opera House and performs *The Nutcracker* every December. As one would expect from such a flamboyant city, the ballet company also excels in innovative performances that would shock the tutus off traditionalists back east.
☎ 865-2000
🖥 www.sfballet.com
✉ War Memorial Opera House, 301 Van Ness Ave
🕙 box office noon-6pm performance days
Ⓜ Civic Center
🚆 K, L, M, N lines to Van Ness, 5, 21, 47, 49 ♿

San Francisco Opera
(5, A7) San Franciscans have loved opera since the Gold

Opera tradition thrives at the War Memorial Opera House

Rush, and the city's opera company presents traditional and new work like the 2001 production of *A Streetcar Named Desire*. Standing room tickets go on sale two hours before performances.
☎ 864-3330
🖥 www.sfopera.com
✉ War Memorial Opera House, 301 Van Ness Ave
🕙 box office 10am-6pm Mon-Fri Ⓜ Civic Center
🚆 K, L, M, N lines to Van Ness, F line, 5, 21, 47, 49 ♿

San Francisco Symphony
(5, A7) The San Francisco Symphony, under the direction of Michael Tilson Thomas, presents old favorites and new music at the Davies Symphony Hall from September to May.
☎ 864-6000
🖥 www.sfsymphony.org
✉ 201 Van Ness Ave
🕙 box office 10am-6pm Mon-Fri, noon-6pm Sat
Ⓜ Civic Center 🚆 K, L, M lines to Van Ness, F line, 5, 21, 47, 49 ♿

GAY & LESBIAN SAN FRANCISCO

Café (4, A2) Twinkies (mainly 20-somethings) are stockpiled for safe keeping in this outgoing dance club. The party often spills out onto a tiny balcony for late-night cat calling to pedestrians.
☎ 861-3846 ✉ 2367 Market St 🕙 2pm-2am Mon-Fri, noon-2am Sat & Sun 🚆 K, L, M lines to Castro, F line, 24, 35, 37 ♿ no

Detour (4, A2) Dark and cruisey, this long-running meat market has several viewing spots – by the pool

table or more provocatively along the chain link fence. Cheap happy hour specials mean everyone is double fisting (drinks, that is), and Sunday after parties usually wrap up here.
☎ 861-6053 ✉ 2348 Market St 🕙 2pm-2am
🚆 K, L, M lines to Castro, F line, 24, 35, 37 ♿

Eagle Tavern (5, B9)
Leather studs, bears, rock-a-billy goats and the straight samplers head to the Eagle on Sunday for the afternoon beer bust. Leather accessories are on sale inside, in

case you forgot your chaps, and there's lots of parking for motorcycles.
☎ 626-0880 ✉ 398 12th St 🕙 noon-2am
🚆 9, 12, 47 🅿 free ♿

El Rio (4, C4) For chiquitas, bananas and mixed fruits, El Rio does a fabulous job of transporting fog dwellers to more tropical climes on Salsa Sundays. Dance lessons precede the onset of cloud-dancers and two-left-footers as the bongos and the sunny day makes everyone communally giddy. Get here early (by 3:30pm) or

risk hearing all the fun from a sidewalk queue.
- ☎ 282-3325
- 🖥 www.elriosf.com
- ✉ 3158 Mission St
- $ cover varies
- 🕓 5pm-2am Mon-Thu, 3pm-2am Fri-Sun
- Ⓜ 24th St 🚌 14, 26 ♿

Esta Noche (4, C2) Amid the straight grazing bars in the Mission, this bimbo dressed in silver and purple is a favorite of the young Latino crowd. Weekend drag shows, salsa music and American Top 40 create an alternate universe of merged cultures.
- ☎ 861-5757
- ✉ 3079 16th St
- 🕓 2pm-2am Ⓜ 16th St
- 🚌 14, 22, 26, 49 ♿

Lexington Club (4, C2) The only full-time lesbian bar in the city is often referred to as the 'home of the homely.' More accurately, it is a forth-right bar for 20-somethings who like pool, cheap beer and working the crowd.
- ☎ 863-2052
- ✉ 3464 19th St
- 🕓 3pm-2am Ⓜ 16th St
- 🚌 14, 26, 49 ♿

Martuni's (6, C5) This cocktail and piano bar draws big crowds with its big, strong drinks, lively conversation and occasional sing-along. A healthy mix of straights and gays enjoy toasting the piano man.
- ☎ 241-0205
- ✉ 4 Valencia St 🕓 4pm-2am 🚌 F line, 26 ♿

Stud (5, B8) Hip young guys have made the Stud their preferred spot to drink and dance for almost 30 years. Lots of funky theme nights, Trannyshack Tuesdays and hip-hop Fridays, keep the bodies fresh.
- ☎ 863-6623
- ✉ 399 9th St
- 🕓 5pm-2am 🚌 12 ♿

Theater Rhinoceros (4, C2) The only theater in San Francisco that is dedicated to performances by, of and for the gay and lesbian community has two stages. You can expect more substance and, less flesh than other similar stage shows. All ages are welcome.

Girl Stuff

The gay capital of the US has only one full-time lesbian bar, it is confounding but true. Instead lesbians mingle with the boys at the **Café** (opposite) and **Stud** (above). Dyke nights at different venues make the pickings easier, check out Kandy Bar Saturday night at the **Endup** (p85), Friday night at the **Stud** and El Rio (opposite) on certain Saturdays.

☎ 861-5079 ▢ www
.therhino.org ✉ 2926
16th St ⏱ box office
1-6pm Wed-Sun Ⓜ 16th
St 🚌 14, 22, 49 ♿

Twin Peaks Tavern (4, A2)
The first gay bar to have
unobscured windows,
Twin Peaks Tavern allowed
the world to look in and
further defined the Castro

as a safe zone. Today, the
wrap-around windows
are less significant for the
younger generation who
refer to it as the glass
coffin. The old-timers
inside are unphased as the
view of the street life is a
rewarding parade.
☎ 864-9470 ✉ 401
Castro St ⏱ noon-2am
🚌 F line ♿

Wild Side West (4, C5)
Considered the best lesbian
bar for everyone, this neighborhood favorite sports
a saloon swagger and a
rambling, tiered garden
filled with plastic junk art,
toilet bowl planters and lots
of nooks and crannies.
☎ 647-3099
✉ 424 Cortland Ave
⏱ 1pm-2am 🚌 24 ♿

SPORTS

In sports, as in music and food, San Francisco proves its sophistication.
Whereas most major league sports are the domain of the American working
class, San Francisco's sports fans are more likely to hail from corporate ranks
rather than unions, making for a more subdued and fashion-conscious
audience. For American grit, you'll have to head to Oakland, where the
cheering (and roughhousing) crowd works just as hard as the athletes.

Scoring tickets for good seats can be a challenge, especially if the team
is in a winning streak. Bleacher seats are almost always available with a
few week's advance reservation. Visit the team's website for availability
and purchase information.

FOOTBALL

The mediocre San Francisco 49ers
still garner support from loyal fans
opposed to crossing the Bay for
their football addiction. The 49ers
play at **Candlestick Park** (☎ 656-
4900; www.sf49ers.com; on I-101
south of San Francisco), the renamed 3Com Park. Like clockwork,
the fog rolls right into Candlestick
on game nights, so come dressed
for frigid weather.

The bad boys of pro football,
the Oakland Raiders, have muscled
their way to the SuperBowl several

Oakland Coliseum, across the bay

Ticket Agencies

TIX Bay Area (5, C5; ☎ 433-7827; www.theatrebayarea.org; Union Sq; ⏱ 11am-
6pm Tue-Fri, 10am-7pm Sat, 10am-3pm Sun) sells half-price tickets to performances
at local theaters on the day of the show. It also sells full-price tickets in advance.
BASS (www.tickets.com) is the 800-pound gorilla of the ticket business, with
outlets at Tower Records and other spots across the Bay Area. **Mr Ticket** (6, C3;
☎ 292-7328; www.mrticket.com; 2065 Van Ness Ave; ⏱ 9am-5:30pm Mon-Fri,
10am-2pm Sat) is worth a venture if your heart is set on a sold-out event.

times but haven't managed to clinch the title since 1984. Their die-hard fans epitomize the pirate mascot with their rabblerousing behavior; be sure to wear lots of black and steer clear of the opposing teams' colors. The Raiders play at the **Oakland Coliseum** (☎ 510-569-2121; www .raiders.com; 7000 Coliseum Way). Contact www.tickets.com for single-game attendance.

College football is almost as popular as the pro variety, particularly the weekend before Thanksgiving, when the **Stanford Cardinals** (☎ 800-782-6367; http://gostanford.collegesports.com) meet the **Cal (UC Berkeley) Bears** (☎ 800-462-3277; www.calbears.com) in the Big Game. The game alternates between Palo Alto (odd years) and Berkeley (even years).

BASEBALL

The Bay Area is blessed with two major league baseball teams, famous for their 1989 face-off in the World Series that was delayed by the Loma Prieta earthquake. The National League San Francisco Giants play at **SBC Park** (formerly Pacific Bell Park; see p24). Tickets can be scarce, but try the Giants website (www.sfgiants.com) at the beginning of the season (early April) for greater options.

The American League Oakland Athletics, the A's, play at the **Oakland Coliseum** (☎ 510-762-2255; www.oaklandathletics.com; on I-880 at 66th Ave), less than 30 minutes by BART (Oakland Coliseum station) from most parts of San Francisco. Tickets can be easier to come by and the weather is more evocative of baseball weather than chilly San Francisco.

Tickets are hard to come by when the San Francisco Giants play at SBC Park

Sleeping

San Francisco's hotels cultivate in two major petri dishes – Union Square and Fisherman's Wharf – tucking in the business and leisure travelers, respectively. While location might seem like everything, this compact city affords a lot of flexibility, opening up its charming neighborhoods as feasible lodging options. Situated a heart-pounding walk from downtown, Nob Hill is littered with historic hotels boasting vaulted ceilings, crown moulding and other architectural details from an embellished past. If you're free of downtown obligations, venture out to the western part of the city where B&Bs and small inns occupy converted houses run by affable proprietors. In the neighborhoods, you'll temporarily join in the daily routine where mommies and skaters wheel in and out of the local coffee shop, the local homeless person attends to mysterious tasks, and teenagers will wait 15 minutes for a bus to take them one block up a hill.

The average room rate is about $155, with some seasonal variations (lowest in January and February, highest from mid-September to mid-November when business travel is at its peak). Rates do fall off on weekends, less so during the prime vacation time of July to August. You can find rooms for under $100, but typically these are in the European B&B style with shared bathroom. Parking is usually available at a nearby garage for $15 to $45 a day. Most hotels have all the mod cons, but smoking in the rooms is usually banned or severely limited.

You can book a room for many hotels through **Topaz Hotel Services** (☎ 800-677-1550; www.hotelres.com). Helpful user reviews of hotels are posted at **Trip Advisor** (www.tripadvisor.com). There are scores of B&Bs scattered around the city. **Bed & Breakfast San Francisco** (☎ 899-0600; www.bbsf.com) and **California B&B Travel Directory** (www.bbtravel.com) represent San Francisco properties.

Most hotels adhere to the federal standards for wheelchair accessibility, but the older hotels without elevators or outfitted rooms have been noted in the review. Children of all ages are welcome at all hotels unless otherwise noted.

DELUXE

Campton Place Hotel (5, C5) Refined and intimate, Campton Place has sleek rooms with a pear wood panelled foyer, large European-style soak tubs, and Egyptian cotton sheets on a fluffy bed. With service the Swiss would envy, the hotel provides complimentary shoe shine and a personable rapport. In-room high-speed Internet, rooftop gym, pet-friendly.
☎ 781-5555 🖳 www.camptonplace.com ✉ 340 Stockton St Ⓜ Montgomery St 🚌 2, 3, 4, 30, 45 Ⓟ $40 ♿ ✖ Campton Place Restaurant (p67)

Clift Hotel (5, B6) Form over function maestro Ian Schrager has invaded San Francisco with another 'in-the-know' creation. Designed to look like a foggy sunset – gray carpet, lavender walls and tangerine highlights – the Clift is creative and fun, but standard rooms are too cramped and the lack of dresser drawers only works for those who buy new clothes every day. In-room wireless, business center, gym.
☎ 775-4700, 800-652-5438 🖳 www.clifthotel.com ✉ 495 Geary St Ⓜ Powell St 🚌 38 Ⓟ $40 ♿ ✖ Asia de Cuba (☎ 929-2300)

Four Seasons (5, C6) This confident, corporate number has sunny rooms with excellent views and deep soak tubs. Best of all, Sports Club LA is the on-site gym (and one of the city's best) boasting NBA-sized courts, a large lap pool and exercise classes. In-room high-speed Internet, 24-hour business center, pet-friendly.
☎ 633-3000, 800-332-3442 🖳 www.fourseasons.com ✉ 757 Market St Ⓜ Powell & Montgomery Sts 🚌 F line, 6, 21 Ⓟ $35 ♿ ✖ Seasons Restaurant (☎ 861-2682)

Mandarin Oriental (5, D4) Classy and sophisticated, the Mandarin Oriental turns a business trip into a vacation. The hotel's towers are linked by observation decks garnering a wide embrace of the city. The rooms boast Asian decor imported straight from a Westchester County living room. In-room high-speed Internet, 24-hour business center, gym and pool, pet-friendly.
☎ 276-9888, 800-622-0404 🖳 www.mandarinoriental.com ✉ 222 Sansome St Ⓜ Embarcadero or Montgomery St 🚌 California St cable car, 10, 15 Ⓟ $36 ♿ ✖ Silks (☎ 986-2020)

Refined and intimate sums up the Campton Place style

TOP END

Archbishiop's Mansion (6, B5) Like stepping into a Jane Austen novel, this 1904 French chateau is ceremonially draped with rich Gothic interiors, exquisite antiques and San Francisco's inimitable informality. Named after famous operas, individually decorated rooms define romance with canopied beds and fireplaces; suites elaborate with claw foot tubs and gracious parlors.
☎ 563-7872, 800-543-5820 🖳 www.thearch bishopsmansion.com ✉ 1000 Fulton St 🚌 5, 21, 22 🅿 free 🚻 🍴 Alamo Square Grill (6, B5; ☎ 440-2828; 803 Fillmore St)

Argonaut Hotel (5, A2) Think *Love Boat* with attention deficit disorder, then you've got the bold nautical theme of this Fisherman's Wharf newcomer. The hotel can accommodate groups, but the in-room Starbucks coffee and a wine hour add an 'inn' ambience. There are also tall rooms outfitted for the Yao Mings of the world. In-room high-speed Internet, wireless in lobby, business center, gym, pet-friendly.
☎ 563-0800, 800-790-1415 🖳 www.argonaut hotel.com ✉ 495 Jefferson St 🚌 F line, 10, 30, 47 🅿 $35 🚻 🍴 Blue Mermaid Chowder House (☎ 771-2222)

Fairmont (5, A4) Maybe it is the hike to the city's ceiling that makes this hotel seem excessively grand. Marble spreads across the floor like spilled milk, columns of gold sprout from the floor to ceiling like palm trees. Dating back to 1907, the Fairmont maintains its older wing, but has transitioned nicely into a new wing with impressive views. In-room high-speed Internet, wireless in lobby, gym and pool, pet-friendly.
☎ 772-5000, 800-441-1414 🖳 www.fairmont .com ✉ 950 Mason St 🚋 California St cable car 🅿 $45 🚻 🍴 Laurel Court, Tonga Room (p83)

Hotel Griffon (5, E4) Just a briefcase toss from the bay, Hotel Griffon is a small 62-room hotel modestly decorated with exposed brick walls, window seats (some with water views) and marble vanities. The executive suites have a small terrace. In-room high-speed Internet, wireless in lobby, business center, gym.
☎ 495-2100, 800-321-2201 🖳 www.hotel griffon.com ✉ 155 Steuart St Ⓜ Embarcadero 🚋 F line, 2, 9, 14, 21, 71 🅿 $24 🚻 🍴 Tonno Rosso (☎ 495-6500)

Hotel Monaco (5, B6) An exuberant Carnaval atmosphere holds court in this Theater District hotel popular with conventioneers and boisterous families. Generous-sized rooms have big screen TVs and garish eye-opening colors. In-room high-speed Internet, wireless in lobby, business center, pet friendly.
☎ 292-0100, 800-214-4220 🖳 www.monaco-sf .com ✉ 501 Geary St Ⓜ Powell St 🚌 38 🅿 $35 🚻 🍴 Grand Café (☎ 292-0101)

Hotel Triton (5, C5) Whimsical and flashy, this hotel is a college dorm on an expense account. Afternoon

Marbled opulence in the lobby of the Fairmont hotel

tarot card readings, wine hour – escape the rat race and take a walk on the wild side. Rooms are individually decorated in honor of San Francisco personalities, such as Jerry Garcia and Santana. In-room wireless, business center, pet-friendly.
☎ 394-0500, 800-800-1299 🖳 www.hoteltriton.com ✉ 342 Grant Ave Ⓜ Montgomery St 🚌 2, 3, 4, 15 Ⓟ $35 🚫 ✕ Café de la Presse (5, C5; ☎ 249-0900; 469 Bush St)

Huntington Hotel (5, B5)
Power and privilege prefer the privacy of this old money legend atop Nob Hill. Spacious apartment-style rooms give refuge to dignitaries, actors and opera stars and bestow glorious views. The exceptional service is professional and welcoming. In-room high-speed Internet, business center, gym and pool.
☎ 474-5400, 800-227-4683 🖳 www.huntingtonhotel.com ✉ 1075 California St 🚋 California St cable car, 1 Ⓟ $35 🚫 ✕ Big 4 (☎ 771-1140)

Nob Hill Lambourne (5, C5) This small walk-up inn is so personable that business travelers and families find it a sweet home away from home. All the beds are hand sewn with organic linens washed with chemical-free soap. The suites have terraces and kitchenettes, but the ground-floor rooms are a little dark. In-room high-speed Internet.
☎ 433-2287, 800-275-8466 🖳 www.nobhill

lambourne.com ✉ 725 Pine St 🚋 Powell-Hyde & Powell-Mason cable cars, 30, 45 Ⓟ $37 🚫 no ✕ Café de la Presse (see Hotel Triton p98)

Pan Pacific Hotel (5, B5)
If the shopping mall aesthetic of the 1980s ever enjoys a revival, this hotel will bask in retro glamor. Until then, we'll just call it ugly. King beds, huge bathroom sinks for messy face washers, flat screen TVs and views from the ninth floor and up – the reliable rooms are disappointingly quirk free. In-room high-speed

A bird's eye view of the Pan Pacific Hotel's retro glamour

Internet, business center, gym, pet-friendly.
☎ 771-8600, 800-553-6465 🖳 www.panpacific.com ✉ 500 Post St Ⓜ Powell St 🚋 Powell-Hyde & Powell-Mason cable cars, 2, 3, 4 Ⓟ $45 🚫 ✕ Pacific Restaurant (☎ 929-2053)

Prescott (5, B5) This 1920s hotel was restored in an Englishmen's club style of overstuffed chairs, Ralph Lauren paisleys and lots of complimentaries if you're in the 'club level.' It's also the home of Wolfgang Puck's Postrio restaurant,

and guests get preferred seating. Business center, gym, pet friendly.
☎ 563-0303, 800-283-7322 ⌨ www.prescotthotel.com ✉ 545 Post St Ⓜ Powell St 🚋 Powell-Hyde & Powell-Mason cable cars, 2, 3, 4 Ⓟ $40 ♿ ✖ Postrio (☎ 776-7825)

Sir Francis Drake Hotel (5, C5) Art deco at its gaudiest with a movie-set lobby and Beefeater doormen, the Drake is an aging star relying on tricks, like history and location, to stay in the spotlight. The rooms are small with worn out bathrooms, worth it if you can score a discounted rate. In-room wireless, business center, gym, pet friendly.
☎ 392-7755, 800-227-5480 ⌨ www.sirfrancisdrake.com ✉ 450 Powell St Ⓜ Powell St

🚋 Powell-Hyde & Powell-Mason cable cars, 2, 3, 4 Ⓟ $40 ♿ ✖ Scala's Bistro (5, C5 ☎ 395-8555; 432 Powell St)

W Hotel (5, D6) For teething capitalists, this W Hotel is both restrained and sensible – like a good pair of chinos – compared to other W indoctrinated facilities. Some of the rooms sneak a peak at the Bay Bridge, and the lobby is filled with an inordinate amount of PIB (people in black). In-room high-speed Internet, wireless in lobby, business center, 24-hour gym.
☎ 777-5300, 877-946-8357 ⌨ www.whotel.com ✉ 181 3rd St Ⓜ Montgomery St 🚌 10, 15, 30, 45 Ⓟ $45 ♿ ✖ XYZ Restaurant (☎ 817-7836)

The sensible W Hotel

MID-RANGE

Hotel Beresford Arms (5, B5) A former apartment building, the Beresford Arms retains a perceptible connection to the days when WWII vets flooded the city with youthful enthusiasm. From your room's bay window, you can feel a newcomer's sense that anything is possible. The operation here is simple and forthright, and rooms are just as honest.
☎ 673-2600, 800-533-6533 ⌨ www.beresford.com ✉ 701 Post St 🚌 2, 3, 4, 38 ♿ ✖ Shalimar (p69)

Hotel Boheme (5, C3) This neighborhood gem is a mix of Parisian romance and North Beach artiness. Emerald and ochre colors decorate the walk-up, along with photos of old jazz and Beat haunts. The rooms are filled with lace canopy beds and old-fashioned phones (showers only, no tubs). And the staff are full of insider suggestions. In-room dial-up.
☎ 433-9111 ⌨ www.hotelboheme.com ✉ 444 Columbus Ave 🚌 15, 30, 41, 45 Ⓟ $31 ♿ no ✖ Mario's Bohemian Cigar Store Café (p73)

Hotel Rex (5, B5) A salon sophistication infuses this quiet Union Square creation. All dolled up with extras like in-room writing desks and a lounge perfect for sipping a Campari or two, the bohemian imagination is further indulged. In-room high-speed Internet, 24-hour business center.
☎ 433-4434, 800-433-4434 ⌨ www.thehotelrex.com ✉ 562 Sutter St Ⓜ Powell St 🚋 Powell-Hyde & Powell-Mason cable cars, 2, 3, 4 Ⓟ $35 ♿ ✖ Café Adrée (☎ 217-4001)

Majestic Hotel (6, C3)
The city's oldest continually operated hotel was built as a private residence in the early 20th century and survived the 1906 earthquake and fire. It retains the sensibility of that time with modern conveniences for guests of this time – the best of both worlds. In-room wireless, gym.
☎ 441-1100, 800-869-8966 ⌨ www.thehotel majestic.com ✉ 1500 Sutter St 🚌 2, 3, 4, 47, 49 Ⓟ $25 ♿

York Hotel (5, A5) An austere marble lobby greets you at this old Union Square haunt. If there were

Drive-In Motels

If you're passing through the city on a road trip and have to deal with a car, you may want to consider one of the roadside motels that line Lombard St from Van Ness Ave to the Presidio, or one of the newer (OK, 1960s and 1970s) motels you'll find in South of Market along Harrison and 7th Sts.

a flashing neon sign out front, you might recognize this as the Empire Hotel from – *Vertigo*. In-room dial-up, gym, pet-friendly.

☎ 885-6800, 800-808-9675 ⌨ www.yorkhotel .com ✉ 940 Sutter St 🚌 2, 3, 4 Ⓟ $35 ♿ ✗ Shalimar (p69)

BUDGET

Andrews Hotel (5, B5)
Just two blocks west of Union Square, this hotel has small but comfortable rooms. The services are equivalent to hotels that are much, much bigger. In-room high-speed Internet.
☎ 563-6877, 800-926-3739 ⌨ www.andrews hotel.com ✉ 624 Post St Ⓜ Powell St 🚌 Powell-Hyde & Powell-Mason cable cars, 2, 3, 4, 38 Ⓟ $28 ♿ ✗ Fino Bar & Restaurant (☎ 928-2080)

Beck's Motor Lodge (6, B6)
A funny anachronism – this 1950s motor lodge sits in the middle of the Castro like a lost suburbanite. Its charmlessness verges on charming and the rooms are straightforward motel issue. Its convenient location is simply unbeatable for

Castro festivals; book early. Pet-friendly.
☎ 621-8212, 800-227-4360 ✉ 2222 Market St 🚌 K, L, M lines to Castro, 24, 37 Ⓟ free ♿ ✗ Café Flore (p63)

Globe Hostel (5, B8)
Rockers and clubbers (from out of state) will find kindred night owls at this hostel near South of Market's club zone with late night jam sessions and pool tables. Average five-bed, unisex dorms (with yucky in-room bathrooms) pass the test as post-drinking crash pads. No full kitchen, lobby Internet access, roof deck, open 24 hours.
☎ 431-0540 ✉ 10 Hallam St, off Folsom St btwn 7th & 8th Sts 🚌 12, 14 ♿ ✗ Tú Lan (p78)

Hostelling International San Francisco Downtown (5, B6) Location, location, location. One block off Union Square, a half-block from the Geary St theaters, this hostel has four-bed dorms (some with and some without inside bathrooms) and private singles and doubles. There are also organized trips to Yosemite and Napa Valley. No full kitchen, lobby Internet access, open 24 hours.
☎ 788-5604, 800-909-4776 ⌨ www.norcal hostels.org ✉ 312 Mason St Ⓜ Powell St 🚌 Powell-Hyde & Powell-Mason cable cars, 5, 21, 38 Ⓟ $15 ♿ ✗ Blondie's (p67)

Hostelling International San Francisco City Center (5, A6) This historic hotel has made a graceful transition to a plush hostel with clean two-, four- and five-bed dorms (in-room bathrooms). The gracious common spaces retain the charm of a hotel lobby. Only the Dashiell Hammett landscape outside is a drawback and requires hard-boiled street smarts. Kitchen privileges, lobby wireless, free walking tours and storage facilities. ☎ 474-5721, 800-909-4776 🖥 www.norcal hostels.org ✉ 685 Ellis St Ⓜ Powell St 🚇 Powell-Hyde & Powell-Mason cable cars, 19, 31 🗶 Mel's Drive-In (p75)

Hostelling International San Francisco-Fisherman's Wharf (6, B1)

At Fort Mason, this hostel has 150 beds in four- to 24-bed dorms that still feel like army barracks, but with a view. Kitchen, open 24 hours, lobby Internet access.

☎ 771-7277, 800-909-4776 🖥 www.norcal hostels.org ✉ Bldg 240, McDowell Ave, Fort Mason 🚌 30 🅿 free, limited 🚻 🗶 Café Franco (☎ 771-7277)

Phoenix Hotel (5, A6)

This 1950s motel has been converted into a rock and roll groupie with a courtyard swimming pool and sun deck hosting almost- and have-been-famous types and their entourages. The rooms are mid-century concoctions with tropical accents – a little bit of Los Angeles in the midst of seedy Tenderloin.

☎ 776-1380, 800-248-9466 🖥 www.sftrips.com ✉ 601 Eddy St 🚌 19, 31 🅿 free 🚻 🗶 Banh Mi Saigon (p66)

Red Victorian Bed, Breakfast & Art (2, F2)

Recovering or born-too-late hippies can indulge in a wad-

ing pool version of communal living at this B&B run by the cosmic Sami Sunchild. The restored Victorian is decorated with her psychedelic peace and love art and flower-child theme rooms, ranging from rainbows to peacocks. Some rooms share a bath. In-room wireless.

☎ 864-1978 🖥 www .redvic.com ✉ 1655 Haight St 🚇 N line, 6, 7, 33, 43, 66, 71 🅿 $20 🚻 🗶 Citrus Club (p69)

San Remo Hotel (5, B2)

Like visiting a spinster aunt, San Remo occupies a walk-up filled with Victorian lace and hanging houseplants. All rooms have shared baths with brass pull-chain toilets and claw-foot tubs. Rooms are decorated with other sensible antiques, without phones or TVs.

☎ 776-8688, 800-352-7366 🖥 www.sanremo hotel.com ✉ 2237 Mason St 🚌 Powell-Mason cable car, 30 🅿 $14 🚻 no 🗶 Mario's Bohemian Cigar Store Café (p73)

Seal Rock Inn (2, A1)

More a motel than a hotel, Seal Rock is a low-key escape to the beach (fog, foghorns and all). Hunter S Thompson used to stay here to listen to the seals, which have since migrated to Fisherman's Wharf. The namesake rock, Cliff House, Sutro Baths and Ocean Beach are all within walking distance.

☎ 752-8000, 888-732-5762 🖥 www.sealrockinn .com ✉ 545 Point Lobos Ave 🚌 38 🚻 🗶 Seal Rock Inn Restaurant (☎ 386-6518)

Relive the summer of love at the Red Victorian

About San Francisco

HISTORY

Small groups of Native Americans lived on the fog-bound peninsula before Spanish empire builders spotted the potential port during an overland expedition in 1769. The Spanish arrived for good in 1776, building a fort (Presidio, p21) and a mission (Mission Dolores, p19). The Ohlone Indians moved into the mission, but few survived once they were exposed to Old World diseases. Mexican officials replaced the Spanish in 1821, but little else changed until 1846, when the Americans captured the fort in a tiny sideshow of the Mexican War.

The City That Was Never a Town

Renamed San Francisco, the outpost was catapulted out of obscurity by the discovery of gold along the American River near Sacramento. By 1849, word was out that there was gold in them there hills and the rush was on. The settlement exploded from 800 people in early 1847 to almost 100,000 in late 1849. Pick-axes, blue jeans and gold-hungry miners flowed out of the city, while new fortunes returned to be squandered on the sins only money could buy. Lawless and hedonistic, the city experienced another boom in 1859 when Henry Comstock discovered his silver lode. This concentrated wealth ushered in a gilded age for the maturing city with the addition of Nob Hill mansions, a showpiece hotel (Palace Hotel) and a civic park (Golden Gate Park, p14–15). By 1900, San Francisco was the capital of the American West, the ninth-largest city in the country with 400,000 residents.

Earthquake & Fire

At 5:12am on April 18, 1906, the great quake struck, estimated at 8.25 on the Richter scale. Hundreds, perhaps thousands, were killed by collapsing buildings. The city's water system was smashed, leaving the remaining buildings and residents defenseless against the ensuing fires that burned almost everything from Mission Dolores north and east to the bay. The Mission Dolores was saved by a miracle when water appeared from a hydrant on the third day after the quake. The 1906 fire exacted more damage than the 1871 Chicago or the great 1666 London fire.

A big earthquake occurred in October 1989 and destroyed parts of the Marina District

Recovery & the New Jerusalem

San Francisco was rebuilt quickly and it celebrated by hosting a world fair, the Panama-Pacific Exposition in 1915. The city retained its title as financial capital of the West but began losing ground to Los Angeles in the 1920s. The attack on Pearl Harbor transformed the city into a WWII staging ground for the Pacific theater. Millions of workers came to work in shipyards and defense plants, or passed through on their way to battle. The wartime boom ran almost 50 years, until cutbacks in defense spending after the collapse of the Soviet Union.

With postwar peace and prosperity, the city's enduring legacy as a safe haven for misfits came to national attention. Bohemian artists, collectively known as the Beats, arrived in North Beach in the 1950s, followed by the Haight-Ashbury hippies in the 1960s. Gay men and lesbians gathered in the Castro to create a community and a movement in the 1970s. The city once again claimed its unconventional title in 2004 when the mayor announced that the city would marry same-sex couples in defiance of a prohibitive California law. Although the courts intervened, San Francisco is always eager to take up the cause of civil disobedience.

Executive Order 9066

In 1942, one year after Pearl Harbor, President Franklin D Roosevelt authorized the alleged security measure of interning all people with Japanese heritage living on the West Coast. In a matter of days San Francisco's Japantown was transformed into a ghost town. Of the 120,000 people who were forcibly relocated to prison-like camps, about two-thirds were American citizens. After the war, the camps were closed and the families returned to find their belongings, homes and businesses gone or usurped.

San Francisco was the financial capital of the west until it lost ground to Los Angeles

Fueled by the technological advances of nearby Silicon Valley, San Francisco rebounded from the 1989 Loma Prieta earthquake and loss of military jobs with the 1990s version of the Gold Rush – the Internet boom. Every bar hosted a launch party, every 20-something was a CEO and San Francisco became a ridiculously expensive place to live. In the aftermath of the Internet crash, only the high cost of living is yet to recede.

ENVIRONMENT

San Francisco is clean by big city standards. Heavy industry is limited, public transport is widespread, and the ocean and bay are clean enough, but not really warm enough, to swim in.

Most of the oceanfront property on the peninsula and Marin Headlands is protected as public parks. In fact, in either direction, there is hardly any place in the Bay Area more than 30 minutes from open spaces.

With all this bounty, it's no accident that the city is a center of environmental consciousness. The Sierra Club was founded here in 1892 and still calls San Francisco home. The prevailing slow growth attitude toward development costs San Franciscans time and money, especially reflected in the cost of housing, but they are generally happy to pay the price.

One of San Francisco's many public parks

GOVERNMENT & POLITICS

In politics as in life, San Francisco marches to its own beat. The city and county is run by the Board of Supervisors, elected from 11 small districts, which allows almost anyone to enter politics. Local officials range from liberal (as in 'just a liberal') to quite left wing ('progressive' in local parlance). The results are sometimes endearing – the city requires companies that do business with the city to provide domestic partner benefits for their unmarried employees and – sometimes infuriating – the city spends $200 million a year on an ineffectual and noncohesive homeless policy.

The best that one can say is San Franciscans genuinely care about their neighbors when residents of other large US cities just want a tax rebate and the homeless off the streets. Alternatively San Franciscans consistently confuse good intentions with good policies, providing right-wing radio talk shows with great material.

ECONOMY

The national downturn and the Internet collapse hit San Francisco's economy hard. But economists predict that the city is poised for a rebound – because the only place left to go is up. The foundation is in place: the local economy is diverse, with technology, energy, retail and finance as major employers, and the workforce is well educated. But the high cost of living thwarts the city's competitive edge and discourages corporate growth, resulting in a higher than average unemployment rate. (Spend some time in a San Francisco coffeeshop and you'll see what an MBA can get you.)

Technology firms (such as Hewlett-Packard, Cisco and Intel) still lead the caravan in the Bay Area, which has been the country's primary technology incubator for the past 50 years. Most of the tech work and almost all the manufacturing actually happens in the South Bay and East Bay suburbs (San Francisco is Silicon Valley's bedroom community).

The city government and tourism are the biggest industries inside the city limits. More than 15 million people visit San Francisco every year, spending an average of $260 each day.

SOCIETY & CULTURE

Thirty years ago, San Francisco was a White, heavily Irish and Italian community with a small percentage of non-White minorities. Today it's the most cosmopolitan small town in the country. Of its 793,633 residents, 43.6% of the population is White, 30% is Asian, 14% Latino and 7.6% African American. In addition, best estimates say at least 11% of city residents, some 80,000 people, are gays or lesbians.

All these different people live together remarkably well. Although San Franciscans tend to live and socialize among their own kind (like people everywhere), they also tend to live next door to many other kinds of

Only in San Francisco

Did You Know?
- The median price of a family home is $555,000
- A one-bedroom apartment in a nice neighborhood will cost about $1500 a month to rent
- The song 'I Left My Heart in San Francisco' was written by a homesick gay couple living in Los Angeles
- San Francisco was built on 43 hills, the steepest with a grade of 31.5%

Da Mayor

This flamboyant city attracts big personalities to vie for the mayoral spot. The present office holder, Gavin Newsom, is as clean cut as they come these days. But he defied the legislature's banning of same-sex marriage, proof that even the city's straight arrows shoot to the left. Before him, Willie Brown, the best dressed man in politics, invited business in through the back door, while exuding the charm of a philandering husband to the anti-corporate populace. Dead Kennedys front man Jello Biafra ran for the seat in 1979 campaigning on the platform that businesspeople should wear clown suits; he came in fourth out of 10. Skipping a campaign, San Francisco resident Joshua Abraham Norton proclaimed himself Emperor of the US in 1819 and outlawed the city's nickname 'Frisco,' a decree observed today.

people. This constant proximity to strangers, and the almost aggressively easygoing attitude, encourages a kind of public civility that masks many surviving prejudices.

The city, however, lacks economic diversity due to the high cost of living. Artists, young families and the working poor have relocated to surrounding suburbs.

Etiquette

This is a friendly city that knows its neighbors and chats to strangers on the bus. It is expected that out-of-towners return the same openness or face being labelled a 'New Yorker.' The city's collective vocabulary outpaces most politically correct standards – 'partner' is used to inquire about significant others, 'diversity' is synonymous with a social utopia and 'protests' or 'rallies' serve the same spiritual function as Sunday church services in other locales.

San Franciscans are sometimes described as passive-aggressive. They'll ask you if you mind that they cut in line or apologize after they steal your parking space. They care, they really do, but not enough to inconvenience themselves – just enough to acknowledge wrong-doing. While their East Coast cousins might shout an obscenity all in the name of social bluntness, San Franciscans tend to avoid personal conflict. Idiosyncratically, they don't practice the same reserve when it comes to sticking it to the so-called man.

ARTS

Where Boston or Chicago support the arts out of virtue, San Francisco supports the arts out of pleasure. There's a broad range of cultural activity here, but little of that earnest 'eat-your-veggies' attitude.

Music

Music has dominated the art scene since the first concert halls went up in the Gold Rush, and today the city enjoys a first-rate opera, as well as a first-rate symphony, led by Michael Tilson Thomas.

Rock and roll, however, looms larger thanks to San Francisco–based legends like the Grateful Dead, Carlos Santana, Janis Joplin and Jefferson Airplane. Punk powers united in nearby Oakland first with the Dead

Music has dominated the San Francisco arts scene since the Gold Rush

Kennedys and later with Green Day. Today the city is obsessed with electronic music (it is the US outpost of drum-and-bass) and guitar revivals. There is a small hip-hop scene, concentrated mainly on freestyle DJs.

Theater & Dance

San Francisco has a small but serious theater scene, dominated by the repertory companies at the American Conservatory Theater (p90), which has launched many famous actors. San Francisco–based playwrights Sam Shepard and Michael McClure helped cement the city's reputation. Small avant-garde theaters dot the Mission and the area around Union Square.

The San Francisco Ballet is the oldest professional ballet company in the USA. Free spirit and San Francisco native Isadora Duncan is widely credited for creating modern dance.

Painting & Visual Arts

Postwar San Francisco manipulated the prevailing painting styles to create such localized expressions as Bay Area figurative and funk art. The San Francisco leaders of abstract expressionism – Clifford Still, Mark Rothko and Frank Lobdell – were challenged by the Bay Area figurative painters – such as Richard Diebenkorn, Elmer Bischoff and David Park – who maintained the same commitment to abstraction but re-introduced lifelike human figures (a no-no in certain circles). Oblivious of conventions,

San Francisco on Film

The airlines have cut in-flight movies for cross-country coach flights, so pack these San Francisco winners for laptop viewing:

- *After the Thin Man* (WS Van Dyke, 1936) Nick and Nora Charles, the tippling detectives, 'summer' in a San Francisco mansion and solve murders on the side.
- *Bullitt* (Peter Yates, 1968) This Steve McQueen thriller contains *the* definitive high-speed car chase.
- *Chan Is Missing* (Wayne Wang, 1982) An indie tour of Chinatown as two friends search for Chan.
- *Crumb* (Terry Zwigoff, 1994) A documentary about San Francisco's favorite underground comic, Robert Crumb.
- *Dirty Harry* (Don Siegal, 1971) Why is Clint Eastwood cool? Because he played this hard-boiled cop who protected the streets of San Francisco.
- *Vertigo* (Alfred Hitchcock, 1958) The quintessential San Francisco movie; see p31.

funk art put the counterculture ideals of the Beat movement into visual art by incorporating collage and painting with pop art aesthetics. Wayne Thiebaud, Mel Ramos and Robert Arneson used the hooks of advertising with a critical artistic message.

San Francisco's natural beauty and surrounding landscape were frequent black-and-white subjects of photographer Ansel Adams.

Mexican Diego Rivera visited the city in the 1930s to produce three social-realist murals (only one is open to the public, see San Francisco Art Institute p34). In the 1980s Mexican muralism took to the streets in the Mission District to curtail vandalism. In the 1990s art school grads added graffiti aesthetics to the tradition to create the Clarion Alley Mural Project (p32), an open-air mural alley. Founding and peripheral members such as Rigo, Barry McGee and Aaron Noble have moved on to international status.

Literature

Political, irreverent and controversial, the city's legendary writers captured city life, collective moods and established a literary tradition for this West Coast publishing leader.

During the Gold Rush, a wry reporter named Mark Twain got his start here. His cross-country stagecoach journey and other frontier stories appeared in *Roughing It*. Cut from the same curmudgeon cloth, Ambrose Bierce (author of *Devil's Dictionary*) worked for the *Examiner* and earned the nickname 'Bitter Bierce.'

Then there were the Beat writers and poets, like Jack Kerouac *(On the Road)* and Allen Ginsberg *(Howl),* who gave voice to rising discontent. Other postwar poets including Kenneth Rexroth *(In What Hour)* and Lawrence Ferlinghetti (owner of City Lights Bookstore and author of *Coney Island of the Mind*) added to the literary scene.

Armistead Maupin's *Tales of the City* books began as a daily column in the *San Francisco Chronicle* and garnered soap opera devotion through the portrayal of straights and gays in the 1970 and '80s.

Amy Tan, author of *The Joy Luck Club*, reveals stories of the narrow Chinatown alleys and culturally sequestered Chinese American families.

The current star in the modern literary scene is Dave Eggers, founder of *McSweeney's* (literary quarterly) and author of *A Heartbreaking Work of Staggering Genius* about the nearly forgotten dot.com days.

Mark Twain and the Beat poets are part of the city's literary success story

Directory

One of the historic and distinctive yellow and orange Market Street trams in the Castro

ARRIVAL & DEPARTURE
Air

There are three major airports that serve San Francisco: San Francisco International (SFO), Oakland International (OAK), and San Jose International (SJC).

SAN FRANCISCO INTERNATIONAL AIRPORT

SFO (1, B2) is on Hwy 101 on the bayside of the peninsula in South San Francisco. It has an international terminal and a domestic terminal. There are no left luggage facilities.

Information

General inquiries ☎ 650-876-2377; www.flysfo.com

Parking information ☎ 650-821-7900

Airline Information

Air Canada ☎ 888-247-2262; www.aircanada.ca

Alaska Airlines ☎ 800-252-7522; www.alaskaair.com

Aloha Airlines ☎ 800-367-5250; www.alohaairlines.com

America West Airlines ☎ 800-235-9292; www.americawest.com

American Airlines ☎ 800-223-5436; www.aa.com

British Airways ☎ 800-247-9297; www.britishairways.com

Continental Airlines ☎ 800-525-0280; www.continental.com

Delta ☎ 800-221-1212; www.delta.com

Japan Airlines ☎ 800-525-3663; www.japanair.com

JetBlue Airways ☎ 800-538-2583; www.jetblue.com

Mexicana ☎ 800-531-7921; www.mexicana.com

Northwest Airlines ☎ 800-225-2525; www.nwa.com

Singapore Airlines ☎ 800-742-3333; www.singaporeair.com

Southwest Airlines ☎ 800-435-9792; www.southwest.com

United ☎ 800-241-6522; www.united.com

Virgin Atlantic ☎ 800-862-8621; www.virgin-atlantic.com

Airport Access

BART (☎ 989-2278; www.bart.gov) trains connect San Francisco International to downtown San Francisco and the East Bay. To reach the airport BART station from any terminal, take the complimentary AirTrain monorail to Garage G/BART station. The trip into downtown takes 30 minutes and costs $5.

Shared vans to downtown can be arranged on a walk-up basis in the Ground Transportation section of each terminal. Reservations are recommended for arrivals after 11pm and for trips to the airport. Companies include **SuperShuttle** (☎ 800-258-3826; www.supershuttle.com) and **SFO Airporter** (☎ 800-282-7758; www.sfoairporter.com). One-way tickets cost around $14 per person.

There are taxi stands in front of each terminal. Fares to downtown locations will run from $30 to $49 for up to five passengers.

OAKLAND INTERNATIONAL AIRPORT

Sometimes flights can be a little cheaper in and out of Oakland International (1, B2), which is about 15 miles east of San Francisco. Its two small terminals handle mainly shuttle flights (including Southwest Airlines) and long distance flights. There are no left luggage facilities here.

Information

General inquiries ☎ 510-577-4000; www.flyoakland.com

Parking information ☎ 510-633-2572, 510-577-5803

Airport Access

AirBart shuttle buses run from the airport terminals to the Coliseum BART station every 15 minutes. The trip takes 10 minutes and costs $2. Buy tickets inside the terminal buildings (inbound) or on the ground level of the BART station (outbound). BART trips into downtown San Francisco take about 25 minutes and cost $3.15.

Taxis are available at stands in front of the terminals. Fares to downtown hotels cost $60 to $65, not including bridge tolls ($2) and tips. A number of private shuttles operate between Oakland and San Francisco and charge from $22 to $40. Call the **Oakland Ground Transportation hotline** ☎ 888-435-9625 for details.

SAN JOSE INTERNATIONAL

The Norman Y Mineta San Jose International Airport is the stepsister of Bay Area airports, about 50 miles south of downtown San Francisco, just a few miles north of downtown San Jose. It's very convenient if you are headed to the South Bay, and not convenient if you are headed anywhere north of Palo Alto. There are no storage lockers here.

Information

General inquiries ☎ 408-501-7600; www.sjc.org

Parking information ☎ 408-277-4759

Airport Access

There is no straightforward transportation between San Francisco and San Jose International besides taxis (about $75) and private cars.

CalTrain (☎ 800-660-4287; www.caltrain.com), the suburban commuter line, stops relatively nearby in Santa Clara and San Jose, close enough to make a connection in a cab.

Train

The grand dame of travel is now an endangered species. Amtrak's *Coast Starlight* stops in Oakland on its run from Los Angeles to Seattle, and the *California Zephyr* ends its journey from Chicago at Emeryville (next door to Oakland). Contact **Amtrak** (☎ 800-872-7245; www.amtrak.com) for fares and schedules. Affiliated shuttle buses will transport customers to and from San Francisco.

CalTrain (☎ 800-660-4287; www.caltrain.com) is the suburban commuter line from San Francisco south to San Jose. The station in San Francisco is at 4th and King Sts (5, E8).

Bus

Greyhound (☎ 800-229-9424; www.greyhound.com) provides nationwide service from its main station at the Transbay Terminal in downtown San Francisco (5, D5; 425 Mission St) and somewhat more limited service from its terminal in downtown Oakland (7, H4; 2103 San Pablo Ave).

Travel Documents
PASSPORT & VISA

Canadians need proof of Canadian citizenship or a passport to enter the US. All other visitors must have a valid passport. Travelers from certain countries can enter the US for up to 90 days under the reciprocal visa waiver program (machine-readable passport required). For the updated list of countries included in this program, visit www.travel.state.gov/vwp.html.

All other travelers will need a visitor's visa. Obtaining visas to enter the US has become more difficult after September 11, 2001; visit the State Department's website (www .unitedstatesvisas.gov) for the most up-to-date regulations. Apply to the US consulate or embassy in your home country as far in advance as possible and be prepared for an in-person interview.

RETURN/ONWARD TICKET

Travelers under the reciprocal visa waiver program will need return or onward tickets to enter the US. Travelers applying for visas overseas will generally require such tickets as proof of their intent to return home.

Customs & Duty-Free

Travelers must specifically disclose all agricultural products and all cash and cash equivalents worth $10,000 or more. Overseas visitors may bring in up to $100 in goods or gifts duty-free, together with 100 cigars, 200 cigarettes and a liter of alcoholic beverages. At the time of writing, Cuban tobacco products were still prohibited in the US.

GETTING AROUND

San Francisco is the one place in California where you can get around without a car. Muni operates the bus and tram system within the city limits; the BART subway system handles some in-town spots en route to the suburbs south and east. Ferries on scenic San Francisco Bay deliver passengers to Tiburon and Sausalito.

San Francisco is laid out in a set of grids mostly running north-south. Market St cuts a diagonal from the piers on the northeast waterfront to the foot of Twin Peaks at the center of the city. Most streets are named, and directions are given with a cross street to help pinpoint the location. Numbered streets run southeast off Market

St, then turn a corner and begin to run east-west through the Mission and the Castro. Forty-eight numbered avenues run coherently north-south across the Richmond and Sunset Districts from the east end of Golden Gate Park out to the beach.

In this book, the nearest BART (**M**) station or Muni (**🚌**) bus or tram line are noted in each listing.

Travel Passes

Muni sells travel passes for one day ($9), three days ($15) and seven days ($20), good on all buses, trams and cable cars; only the express buses to 3Com Park are exempt. Buy travel passes at the cable car turntable at Powell and Market Sts, the San Francisco Visitors Information Center (p122) or at corner stores around town. You can also buy passes at www.sfmuni.com.

Muni

Blamed for everything from lateness to bad hair days, **Muni** (Municipal Railway; ☎ 673-6844; www .sfmuni.com) operates nearly 100 bus lines (many of them electric), light-rail and the famous cable cars. Fares on buses and light-rail are $1.25/$0.35. Cable cars are $3 one-way. Buses take dollar bills (have exact change), only Muni light-rail stations have change machines. Transfers are valid for one ride within 90 minutes of purchase. Service is frequent during rush hour and less reliable at midday and late at night. A quintessential San Francisco moment is waiting for a bus and watching three buses going the other way. The *Street & Transit Map* shows all Muni routes, and can be purchased from the San Francisco Visitors Information Center.

Unique to the system, the historic F line streetcars run from Market and Castro Sts to the waterfront, then north along the waterfront to Fisherman's Wharf (see p13).

The light-rail system operates as a subway through downtown with stations coinciding with BART stations. As the trams extend westward, they emerge to street level. Muni lines are denoted with the 🚌 symbol throughout this book.

BART

The **Bay Area Rapid Transit** (BART; ☎ 989-2278; www.bart.gov) trains serve downtown, the Mission, East Bay, Peninsula suburbs and the airport. Service is fast and dependable. Fares vary based on the length of the trip. A trip from Civic Center to the Mission District is $1.25, while a trip from downtown to Berkeley costs $3.05. BART lines are denoted with the Ⓜ symbol throughout this book.

Ferry

Blue & Gold Fleet Ferries (5, B1; ☎ 705-5555; www.blueandgoldfleet.com; one-way tickets $7-10) operates from the Ferry Building at the foot of Market St and from Pier 41 at Fisherman's Wharf, to Jack London Square in Oakland, Alcatraz, Angel Island and Sausalito.

Taxi

Taxis are usually easy to find in the center of the city and tourist zones. You can hail a taxi on the street, or call **De Soto** (☎ 970-1300), **Veterans** (☎ 552-1300) or **Yellow** (☎ 626-2345). Taxis are harder to come by in the evenings, rainy days and near-impossible on big nights like Halloween or New Year's Eve. Basic charges for rides within the city start at $2.85, and cost an additional $0.45 for each $1/5$ mile.

Car & Motorcycle

You won't need a car to get around San Francisco, but for trips further afield consider a short-term rental. If you need a car in the city, your biggest problem will be parking. Most hotels offer valet services with in and out privileges. There are also 24-hour garages at Sutter & Stockton Sts, Fifth and Mission Sts, and under Union Square, Portsmouth Square and the Civic Center Plaza. Rates typically start at $1 to $2 for the first hour with flat rates ranging from $18 to $25. Parking lots are few and far between outside downtown, and on-street parking in most neighborhoods is limited. If you park on a hill, curb your wheels to keep your car from running away.

ROAD RULES

San Franciscans drive on the right side of the road and you can turn right on a red light after a full stop unless a sign says otherwise. Seat belts are compulsory for all front seat passengers. Children under three must be strapped in safety seats. The basic speed limit in the city is 30mph. Driving under the influence of alcohol or drugs is strictly prohibited (California has a 0.08% blood alcohol limit).

RENTAL

You can rent a car at the airports or in the city. Big national car rental chains, such as **Alamo** (5, B5; 693-0191, 800-327-9633; 750 Bush St) and **Budget** (5, B6; ☎ 800-527-0700; 321 Mason St), are conveniently located. Daily rates range from $15 to $30 and require advance reservations especially for convertibles on busy summer weekends. You must be at least 21 years old to rent a car and at least 25 to avoid a daily surcharge.

DRIVING LICENSE & PERMIT

Canadian and Mexican driving licenses are generally accepted in the San Francisco area. Other overseas travelers should carry their domestic driving licenses and an international driving permit.

Bicycle

Avenue Cyclery (2, E3; ☎ 387-3155; www.avenuecyclery.com; 756 Stanyan St, Haight) and **Blazing Saddles** (5, A2; ☎ 202-8888; www .blazingsaddles.com; 1095 Columbus Ave, North Beach) rent bikes for the hour ($7-$11) and the day ($25-$30).

Motoring Organizations

The **American Automobile Association** (5, A8; ☎ 565-2012, 800-222-4357; www.aaa.com; 150 Van Ness Ave; ☾ 8:30am-5:30pm Mon-Fri), the pre-eminent motoring organization in the US, provides minor breakdown service, short-distance towing, and other acts of mercy. AAA members can also get road maps and discounts from hotels and car rental companies.

PRACTICALITIES
Climate & When to Go

Summer is the busiest time in San Francisco, though it is true that a summer in San Francisco can be one of the coldest winters you'll ever experience. Expect fog and wind in the mornings and late afternoons. Wear layers to accommodate the fickle weather. The best times to visit are in the spring around March, just after the winter rains, or in the warm, dry months of September and October. The winter rainy season, which usually starts late October, can be wet and gloomy, but temperatures never go below freezing and there's always the chance of a warm spell that makes you think you're in Palm Springs.

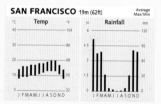

Disabled Travelers

San Francisco is a surprisingly good destination for the mobility impaired. All the Muni trains and buses are wheelchair accessible; for information call ☎ 923-6142. Most of the major sights, hotels and restaurants are also wheelchair accessible. Some older hotels are walk-ups and don't have elevators; those are noted in the reviews.

Mobility International USA (☎ 541-343-1284; www.miusa.org) advises disabled travelers on mobility issues and runs education programs. The **Society for Accessible Travel and Hospitality** (☎ 212-447-7284; www.sath.org; 347 Fifth Ave, Suite 610, New York 10016) publishes *Open World*, a magazine for disabled travelers.

Discounts

Many museums, tours and sights have discount tickets for children and seniors. **CityPass** (www.city pass.net), available at the Visitors Center (p122) offers up to 50% savings on admissions to six of the big attractions in town – the San Francisco Museum of Modern Art (p26), the Blue & Gold Fleet Bay Cruise, the Exploratorium (p39), the Palace of the Legion of Honor (p31), California Academy of Sciences (p39) and Asian Art Museum (p9).

STUDENT & YOUTH CARDS

Most student and teacher discounts are reserved only for students and teachers from local institutions.

SENIORS' CARDS

San Francisco is a popular destination for seniors. The **American Association of Retired Persons** (AARP; ☎ 800-424-3410; www .aarp.org), a lobbying group for Americans 50 years and older, has hotel and car rental discounts for members.

Seniors can get discounts at some sights and hotels. Ask if you don't see a sign. Some discounts apply to persons 50 and over, others to persons 60 or 65 and over. Seniors 65 and over with a photo ID pay reduced fares on Muni vehicles, except the cable cars.

Electricity

Adaptors for European and South American plugs are common. Australians should bring their own adaptors.

Voltage	110V
Frequency	60Hz
Cycle	AC
Plugs	two or three pins (two flat, with an optional round grounding pin)

Embassies or Consulates

Australia (5, D5; ☎ 536-1970; 625 Market St, San Francisco CA 94104)
Canada (5, C4; ☎ 834-3180; 555 Montgomery St, San Francisco CA 94104)
France (5, C5; ☎ 397-4330; 540 Bush St, San Francisco CA 94108)
Germany (6, C3; ☎ 775-1061; 1960 Jackson St, San Francisco CA 94109)
Ireland (5, D4; ☎ 392-4214; 100 Pine St, 33rd fl, San Francisco, CA 94111)
Japan (5, D5; ☎ 777-3533, 50 Fremont St, Suite 2300, San Francisco, CA 94105)
Mexico (5, C6; ☎ 782-9555; 870 Market St, San Francisco CA 94102)

Emergencies

Police, fire, ambulance ☎ 911
Police information ☎ 553-0123
Rape crisis line ☎ 647-7273

Fitness

San Franciscans are annoyingly obsessed with fitness. Gyms and yoga studios are as prolific as juice shops, and daily rates for visitors range from $12 to $20. Golden Gate Park and the Embarcadero are common jogging routes.

Club One (5, D4; ☎ 788-1010; www.clubone.com; 2 Embarcadero Center; ⏱ 5:30am-10pm Mon-Fri, 7am-7pm Sat & Sun; BART Embarcadero; Muni F line, 9) Club One is in eight locations around town and offers all the mod cons.
Embarcadero YMCA (5, E4; ☎ 957-9622; www.ymca.net; 169 Steuart St; ⏱ 5:30am-10pm Mon-Fri, 8am-8pm Sat, 9am-6pm Sun; BART Embarcadero; Muni F line, 2, 7, 9, 14, 21, 71) One of the best YMCA facilities in the country with a full schedule of classes and a sensational indoor pool.
Funky Door Yoga (5, D6; ☎ 957 1088; www.funkydooryoga.com; 186 2nd St; 7am, noon, 4:30pm, 6:15pm Mon-Fri; BART Embarcadero; Muni F line, 9) This place offers classes in Bikram yoga.
Gold's Gym (5, C9; ☎ 552-4653; www.goldsgym.com; 1001 Brannan St; ⏱ 5am-midnight Mon-Thu, to 11pm Fri, 7am-9pm Sat, 8am-8pm Sun; Muni 9) If body image has become a monster of gay male big city life, then Gold's are the belly of the beast.
Harding Park Golf Course (3, B6; ☎ 664-4690; www.hardingparkgolf.com; 1 Harding Rd, Lake Merced; $26-35; ⏱ 6:45am to btwn 5pm & 8pm; Muni 18, 122)

Gay & Lesbian Travelers

Not everyone in San Francisco is gay, but like gentiles in New York City, straight San Franciscans often absorb aspects of the gay culture through osmosis. Gays and lesbians are visible in every walk, and simple gestures like hugs and hand holding are commonplace. Gay bashing and name calling are rare, but not unheard of. Like everyone else in town, gay and lesbian visitors should watch where they walk at night.

The Castro is the heart of the gay and lesbian community, a place to meet or hang out on a sunny afternoon, or to congregate in times of emergency. South of Market is club-land, home to most of the leather bars, and half the dance and sex clubs in town. Polk St still has a strip of bars and clubs, but it's a shadow of its 1970s self.

INFORMATION & ORGANIZATIONS

San Francisco has three gay, free weeklies – the *Bay Area Reporter* and *San Francisco Frontiers,* which focus on community arts and politics, and *Odyssey,* which covers community play.

The **San Francisco Community Center** (6, C5; ☎ 865-5555; www .sfgaycenter.org; 1800 Market St; Muni K, L, M, N lines to Van Ness, F line, 26) is a safe home base for GLBT resident organizations and visitors alike. Check out the view from the 4th-floor deck.

Health
IMMUNIZATIONS

Vaccinations and immunizations are not needed to enter the US.

PRECAUTIONS

You can drink the tap water in San Francisco (it's fresh from the mountains), and you can breathe the air (pollution gets blown away). If you exercise or walk up a lot of hills, drink plenty of fluids; the climate is dry. Wear sunscreen as even the winter sun is strong. The usual precautions apply in the city when it comes to sex. Condoms are available at any pharmacy and most corner stores.

INSURANCE & MEDICAL TREATMENT

Overseas visitors should make sure they have medical insurance before they come to San Francisco. Medical care can be very expensive in the US and many doctors and hospitals insist on payment before treatment.

MEDICAL SERVICES

The **University of California-San Francisco Medical Center** (2, E3; ☎ 476-1000; 505 Parnassus Ave) is one of the country's leading hospitals. **San Francisco General** (3, E4; ☎ 206-8000; 1001 Potrero Ave) is the public hospital and has one of the best trauma units. Other hospitals with 24-hour emergency services include **Davies Medical Center** (4, A1; ☎ 565-6000; Castro & Duboce Sts) and **St Francis Memorial Hospital** (5, A5; ☎ 353-6000; 900 Hyde St).

For HIV-related questions, call the **AIDS Hotline** (☎ 863-2437). For other health questions, try the **Lyon-Martin Women's Health Services** (6, C5; ☎ 565-7667; 1748 Market St). The **Gay & Lesbian Medical Association** (☎ 255-4547; www.glma.org) offers health care referrals.

DENTAL SERVICES

If you chip a tooth, discover a cavity or require emergency dental treatment, contact the **San Francisco Dental Office** (5, E4; ☎ 777-5115; 131 Steuart St; ☺ 8am-4:30pm Mon, Tue & Fri, 10:30am-6:30pm Wed-Thu).

PHARMACIES

Walgreens pharmacies have locations throughout the city, including stores at 730 Market St (5, C5; ☎ 397-4800) and 135 Powell St (5, C6; ☎ 391-4433). There are Rite-Aid stores in several locations, including a downtown store at 776 Market St (5, C6; ☎ 397-0837).

Holidays

Jan 1	New Years Day
Jan	Martin Luther King Jr Day (third Mon)
Feb	President's Day (third Mon)
Mar/Apr	Easter Sunday
May	Memorial Day (last Mon)
Jul 4	Independence Day
Sep	Labor Day (first Mon)
Oct	Columbus Day (second Mon)
Nov 11	Veterans' Day
Nov	Thanksgiving (fourth Thu)
Dec 25	Christmas Day

Imperial System

Americans still use what they call the English system of weights and measures. Distances come in inches, feet, yards and miles; dry weights in ounces, pounds and tons; liquid volumes in pints, quarts and gallons. The US gallon contains about 20% less than the imperial gallon because it only amounts to 4 quarts. See the conversion table below.

TEMPERATURE
$°C = (°F - 32) ÷ 1.8$
$°F = (°C \times 1.8) + 32$

DISTANCE
1in = 2.54cm
1cm = 0.39in
1m = 3.3ft = 1.1yd
1ft = 0.3m
1km = 0.62 miles
1 mile = 1.6km

WEIGHT
1kg = 2.2lb
1lb = 0.45kg
1g = 0.04oz
1oz = 28g

VOLUME
1L = 0.26 US gallons
1 US gallon = 3.8L
1L = 0.22 imperial gallons
1 imperial gallon = 4.55L

Internet

Most cafés offer wireless and terminal Internet access and hotels usually have in-room, high-speed services. Downtown Internet cafés with terminals typically charge around $10 per hour and include **Quetzal** (5, A5; ☎ 673-4181; 1234 Polk St; ⏰ 6am-11pm; Muni 19) or **cafe.com** (5, B6; ☎ 433-4001; 120 Mason St; ⏰ 8am-10pm; BART Powell St). The **Main Library** (5, A7; Hayes & Larkin Sts, Civic Center; BART Civic Center) offers free Internet access.

America Online, Earthlink, Yahoo and Verizon are Internet service providers in San Francisco. For customers of these ISPs, visit their websites or contact customer service for a list of local access numbers.

Useful Sites

The Lonely Planet website (www .lonelyplanet.com) offers a speedy link to many of San Francisco's websites. Others to try include:

www.sfgate.com San Francisco Chronicle

www.sfvisitor.org San Francisco Convention and Visitors Bureau

www.sfbg.com San Francisco Bay Guardian

Lost Property

The Muni lost and found department is located at 2620 Geary Blvd (6, A4; ☎ 923-6168).

Money
ATMS

ATMs are a good alternative to traveler's checks, particularly for overseas visitors. You can find ATMs all over town and most accept cards from the Cirrus, Star and Global Access networks. Charges to use another bank's ATMs usually start at $1.50, but you should check with your home bank about additional charges. San Franciscans observe a unique etiquette regarding cash machines.

They queue for streetside ATMs at the curb, leaving the sidewalk unobstructed. Out-of-towners sometimes line-up directly behind the current customer not realizing that there is an already formed line.

CHANGING MONEY

Banks usually offer better rates than exchange offices. Most major banks will change money during normal business hours. American Express is located at 455 Market St (5, D5; ☎ 536-2600; ⏱ 9am-5pm Mon-Fri, 10am-2pm Sat). Travelex-Thomas Cook has a downtown location (5, C5; ☎ 800-287-7362; 75 Geary St; 9am-5pm Mon-Fri, 10am-4pm Sat) and several currency exchange booths in the international terminal at San Francisco International Airport. Hours vary based on flight schedules. Overseas visitors can also use their ATM cards to get US cash at bank rates almost anywhere.

CREDIT CARDS

Major credit cards are accepted just about everywhere. You will need major credit cards to rent a car, register for a hotel room, or buy tickets to a play or sporting event. Visa and MasterCard are the most commonly accepted. Carry copies of your credit card numbers separately from your cards. If your cards are lost or stolen, contact the company immediately.

American Express	☎ 800-528-4800
Diners Club	☎ 800-234-6377
Discover	☎ 800-347-2683
MasterCard	☎ 800-826-2181
Visa	☎ 800-336-8472

CURRENCY

US dollars are the only currency accepted in San Francisco. The US dollar is divided into 100 cents. Coins come in denominations of $0.01 (a penny), $0.05 (nickels), $0.10 (dimes), $0.25 (quarters), $0.50 (half-dollars) and $1.00 (dollars). Although a new dollar coin was recently issued, one rarely sees dollar coins or half-dollar coins. Quarters are the handiest coins for vending machines, parking meters and bus fares.

US bills are all the same color and size. They come in $1, $2, $5, $10, $20, $50 and $100 denominations, but $2 bills are rare.

Newspapers & Magazines

San Francisco has two daily newspapers – the *San Francisco Chronicle* and the *San Francisco Examiner*. The *Chronicle* has a mixed reputation, to put it charitably. It is very strong on lifestyle coverage and weak on hard news.

San Francisco Magazine is a glossy monthly catering to professionals, filled with restaurant reviews and cultural news. The *Bay Guardian* and *SF Weekly* are free weeklies with strong entertainment coverage, and are available in newsboxes around town. The *BAR* (Bay Area Reporter) and *Frontiers* are free weeklies for the gay and lesbian community.

Opening Hours

The work week runs from 8:30am or 9am to 5pm or 5:30pm Monday to Friday. Banks and post offices typically observe this schedule with abbreviated hours on Saturday. Most shops are open daily, from 10am or 11am to 6pm or 7pm Monday to Saturday, and noon to 6pm on Sundays. Restaurants are usually open daily, from 11:30am to 2pm for lunch and from about 5:30pm to 10pm or 11pm for dinner; weekends typically have extended evening hours. Banks, schools, and post and government offices observe most or all public holidays, while other businesses observe Christmas, New Years and 4th of July.

Photography & Video

For high-end equipment and film, head to **Adolph Gasser** (5, D6; ☎ 495-3852; 181 2nd St; ☺ 9am-6pm Mon-Fri, 10am-4pm Sat). For simpler stuff, try **Brooks Camera** (5, C5; ☎ 362-4708; 125 Kearney St; ☺ 8am-7pm Mon-Sat) or one of the many branches of **Wolf Camera** (4, B1; ☎ 626-4573; 2016 Market St; ☺ 9am-7pm Mon-Fri, 10am-6pm Sat, 11am-6pm Sun). For film processing, try Wolf or **Ritz Camera** (5, B6; ☎ 835-3714; 1 Hallidie Plaza; 9am-6:30pm Mon-Sat, 11am-6pm Sun). Or go to any Walgreens (p117).

Overseas visitors shopping for videos must remember that the US uses the NTSC system, which is incompatible with the PAL (UK and Australasia) and SECAM formats (Western Europe).

Post

There are downtown post offices in the Hallidie Building, 150 Sutter St (5, C5) and Macy's at 170 O'Farrell St (5, C6). See the 'Government Listings' section of the white pages or call ☎ 800-275-8777 for other branches. The US Postal Service's website (www.usps .com) has a list of relevant zip codes. Stamps are sold at post offices, grocery stores and some pharmacies.

POSTAL RATES

Domestic postage rates are $0.37 for letters to 1 oz. ($0.23 each additional oz.) and $0.23 for postcards. International airmail costs are:

Cost ($)	1 oz./2 oz.
Australia, Japan	0.80/1.70
EU	0.80/1.60
Canada	0.60/0.85
Mexico	0.60/0.85

Radio

San Francisco boasts two National Public Radio stations, KQED at 88.5 FM (the most successful National Public Radio outlet in the country) and KALW at 91.7 FM. Noncommercial, community supported radio can be found at KUSF 90.3, from the University of San Francisco, and KPOO 89.5 FM, which broadcasts the Tuesday Board of Supervisor's meetings. For conventional news radio try KCBS at 740 AM. Find oldies on KISS at 99.7 FM, classic rock on KFOG 104.5 FM, classical on KDFC 102.1 FM, Mexican pop at KSOL 98.9 FM and hip-hop on KMEL 106.1 FM.

Safety Concerns

San Francisco isn't always the cool gray city of love. Seedy neighborhoods abound – the Tenderloin (between downtown and Civic Center, roughly from Taylor St to Hyde or Larkin Sts), Market St from 6th to Valencia Sts, and Mission St from 17th up. By and large the druggies, dealers and prostitutes are interested only in potential customers and couldn't care less about accidental visitors. In these neighborhoods, often newcomers' own fear is their worst enemy; if you stumble upon these areas, keep a confident gait and look straight ahead to avoid inviting unsolicited attention. If someone asks you for money in these neighborhoods, give a perfunctory 'sorry,' and keep moving. Don't carry around huge amounts of cash, and watch your belongings on the bus.

Telephone

Public telephones are generally coin-operated, although some pay phones accept phonecards and credit cards. Local calls are generally $0.35. Calls to the suburbs will cost more. The area code for the city of San Francisco and Marin County to the north is ☎ 415. The East Bay suburbs of Oakland and

Berkeley are in area code ☎ 510. SFO and the suburbs on the San Francisco Peninsula are in area code ☎ 650. If you're dialing a number outside the area you're calling from, be sure to dial ☎ 1 first.

PHONECARDS
Phonecards for domestic and international destinations are available in almost every imaginable denomination and can be bought at any corner store.

MOBILE PHONES
The US uses a variety of mobile phone systems, only one of which is a GMS remotely compatible with systems used outside of North America. Most North American travelers can use their mobiles in the San Francisco Bay Area, but they should check with their carriers about roaming charges.

USEFUL NUMBERS
Local directory inquiries ☎ 411
International directory inquiries (AT&T)
☎ 412-555-1515
International dialing ☎ 011
International operator ☎ 00
Reverse charge (collect) ☎ 0
Operator-assisted calls ☎ 01
(then dial the number, an operator will come on after you have dialed)
Traffic ☎ 511

INTERNATIONAL DIRECT DIAL CODES
Australia ☎ 61
Canada ☎ 1
France ☎ 33
Germany ☎ 49
Japan ☎ 81
New Zealand ☎ 64
South Africa ☎ 27
UK ☎ 44

Television
You'll find the usual US suspects on the small screen. Every national network has a local affiliate, including Spanish language Univision (Channel 14). There are three PBS affiliates, KQED (Channel 9), KTEH (Channel 54) and KCSM (Channel 60). The city's public access station is on Channel 29.

Time
San Francisco is in the Pacific Standard Time Zone, which is eight hours behind GMT/UTC. Daylight saving time runs from the first Sunday of April to the last Saturday of October.

At noon in San Francisco it's:
3pm in New York
noon in Los Angeles
8pm in London
9pm in Johannesburg
6am (following day) in Auckland
4am (following day) in Sydney

Tipping
Tipping is customary in bars, restaurants, and hotels. Tip your server at a restaurant 20% (15% if the service was terrible). Tip the bartender $1 for one or two beers, or 15% for a round. Tip taxi drivers $1 on a fare of $6 or less, 10% from there on up. Tip baggage carriers $1 a bag, and valet parkers $2 when they hand you the keys to your car. Doormen should get from $1 to $2 to get you a cab, the concierge at your hotel $5 or more for booking a table or theater tickets, and the maid at your hotel from $1 to $2 a night.

Toilets
You'll find some stand-alone green toilet stalls imported from France scattered around the city streets, but these tend to be frequented by drug addicts. You're better

off sauntering into a big hotel or shopping complex. Haight St is notorious for refusing bathroom access to non-customers, so you might have to buy a drink.

Tourist Information

The **San Francisco Visitors Information Center** (5, B6; ☎ 391-2000; www.sfvisitor.org; 900 Market St; ⌚ 9am-5pm Mon-Fri, to 3pm Sat & Sun; BART Powell St) provides information from maps and brochures about city sights and online hotel reservations, to city guides and a newsletter that you can download for free from its website.

Women Travelers

Women won't experience any abnormal behavior in San Francisco that isn't consistent with the city's wacky personality. Traveling the buses and streets at night in most neighborhoods is safe. If you're in the Mission, avoid eye contact with Latino men on the street who will interpret even a passing glance as an invitation. San Francisco is so enlightened that women are even safe to walk into a bar alone without encountering uninvited come-ons. For health issues, contact **Planned Parenthood** (6, C4; ☎ 800-967-7526; 815 Eddy St).

Index

See also separate indexes for Eating (p126), Sleeping (p125), Shopping (p126) and Sights with map references (p127).

SLEEPING

EATING

SHOPPING

Sights Index

FEATURES

[Sears Fine Food]	**Eating**
[Exit Theater]	**Entertainment**
[The Saloon]	**Drinking**
[Brainwash]	**Café**
[Asian Art Museum]	**Highlights**
[City Lights Bookstore]	**Shopping**
[Cable Car Museum]	**Sights/Activities**
[York Hotel]	**Sleeping**

AREAS

- Beach, Desert
- Building
- Land
- Mall
- Other Area
- Park/Cemetary
- Sports
- Urban

HYDROGRAPHY

- River, Creek
- Intermittent River
- Canal
- Swamp
- Water

BOUNDARIES

- State, Provincial
- Regional, Suburb
- Ancient Wall

ROUTES

- Tollway
- Freeway
- Primary Road
- Secondary Road
- Tertiary Road
- Lane
- Under Construction
- One-Way Street
- Unsealed Road
- Mall/Steps
- Tunnel
- Walking Path
- Walking Trail
- Track
- Walking Tour

TRANSPORT

- Airport, Airfield
- Bus Route
- Cycling, Bicycle Path
- Ferry
- General Transport
- BART/MUNI
- Cable-Car, Funicular
- Monorail
- Rail
- Taxi Rank

SYMBOLS

- Bank, ATM
- Buddhist
- Castle, Fortress
- Christian
- Diving, Snorkeling
- Embassy, Consulate
- Hospital, Clinic
- Information
- Internet Access
- Islamic
- Jewish
- Lighthouse
- Lookout
- Monument
- Mountain, Volcano
- National Park
- Parking Area
- Petrol Station
- Picnic Area
- Point of Interest
- Police Station
- Post Office
- Ruin
- Telephone
- Toilets
- Zoo, Bird Sanctuary
- Waterfall

24/7 travel advice
www.lonelyplanet.com

SHE COME BRINGING ME THAT LITTLE BABY GIRL

by
Eloise Greenfield
Illustrated by
John Steptoe

THIS BOOK IS THE PROPERTY OF:

STATE _____

PROVINCE _____

COUNTY _____

PARISH _____

SCHOOL DISTRICT _____

OTHER _____

Book No. _____

Enter information
in spaces
to the left as
instructed

ISSUED TO	Year Used	CONDITION	
		ISSUED	RETURNED
....	....		
....	....		
....	....		
....	....		
....	....		
....	....		
....	....		
....	....		

PUPILS to whom this textbook is issued must not write on any page
or mark any part of it in any way, consumable textbooks excepted.

1. Teachers should see that the pupil's name is clearly written in ink in the spaces above in every book issued.

2. The following terms should be used in recording the condition of the book: New; Good; Fair; Poor; Bad.